KEY TO
A BASIC COURSE
IN
ENGLISH

A First Dictionary
A First English Companion
A First Encyclopaedia
Comprehension Crosswords
Learn to Spell
Learn Good English
A Beginner's Encyclopaedia
Better Letters
Secondary Comprehension: A Dual Approach

ARE ALSO BY

Walter D. Wright

KEY TO
A BASIC COURSE IN
ENGLISH

by Walter D. Wright

JAMES NISBET AND COMPANY LTD

PUBLISHED BY
JAMES NISBET & COMPANY LIMITED
HITCHIN, HERTS

FIRST PUBLISHED 1961
REVISED 1982

PRINTED AND BOUND IN GREAT BRITAIN BY
BOOKCRAFT BATH LTD
0 7202 0951 X

CONTENTS

The Answers to the 'Mark These Yourself' exercises in *A Basic Course in English* are given on pages 144–146 of the pupils' book.

The references *F. D. & C. Manual* are to those parts of the *Teachers' Manual to A First Dictionary and A First English Companion* which it may be helpful to consult for fuller discussion or further suggestions.

PREFACE

IN my Preface to *A Basic Course in English* I have expressed the opinion that drill and practice in the basic skills of English should be carried out with the greatest possible economy of time. This applies no less to claims upon the teacher than to demands upon the pupil. In compiling this *Key*, therefore, I have given answers even to the simplest exercises, knowing that the busy teacher with a pile of books to mark is glad of a check-list that obviates frequent cross-reference to the text book. Rapid marking of correct answers frees the teacher for the more important task of discussing errors.

There are occasions when the teacher can make good use of additional exercises and examples that are not otherwise accessible to the pupil. With this in mind I have drawn attention to relevant sections of my *Teachers' Manual to A First Dictionary and A First English Companion*, a source of supplementary material that will be found helpful no matter whether these particular books are being used in class or not. The form of cross-reference adopted in this connection can be seen at the foot of page 1; appropriate teaching-notes are similarly indicated.

Knowing how easy it is in the writing and production of books to let the odd error slip through undetected, I make no apology for asking that my attention be drawn to any such oversight in this *Key*.

W.D.W.

Cannock
Staffordshire
1961

Page 1

7. (*b*) East Enders determined to show that they were as loyal as ever.

Youngsters for whom this was a new experience.

And old-age pensioners who wondered if this might be their last chance.

Page 2

7. (*d*) From the doctors, good news.
Coupled with a warning.
And still falling.

4. (*h*) thigh

Page 3

5. (*g*) denim

Page 8 Noun or verb? (illustrated exercise)

(1) to bark (verb); bark (noun)

(2) to skate (verb); a skate (noun)

9. (*a*) *Burmese* teak

(*n*) *Ghanaian* cocoa

Page 12

7. (2) king   queen

Page 17 15.

1. (*f*) During the holiday I read
The Hobbit.

Page 19 16.

1. (*h*) we = Prema and Rashid
they = the squirrels
us = Prema and Rashid

2. (*a*) Who may not be old enough to join the club?
Curtis asked Leroy if he (Curtis) was old enough to join the club. (Or *vice versa*)

Page 23

8. (*g*) The passengers waited *patiently*.

Page 25

4. (*a*) The *oldest* of them all is Tunde.

Page 27

4. (*e*) Our firm is *behind* the times; we still have no computer.

(*m*) He won the V.C. for great bravery while *under* enemy fire.

6. (*f*) She lent me the hose (that) she washes the car *with*.

Page 29

4. (*h*) Neither of the grocers in our village *has* a freezer in *his shop*.

Page 30

8. (*a*) Please keep seats for Amina and *me*.

Page 34

14.(*d*) Mr. Faulkner, *whom the terrorists are holding to ransom*, is a retired civil servant.

Page 35

3. (*f*) Visitors sometimes bring gifts.

Page 39

1. (*h*) A skin (noun)

2.   courageous   courageously   courage

Page 43 28.

1. I eat my peas with honey,
I've done it all my life.
It makes the peas taste funny
But it keeps them on the knife!

Pages 43 and 44 29.

5. or near offer, Old Age Pensioners, Bed and Breakfast, post and packing, Hire Purchase, stamped addressed envelope.

7. Indira Datt, M.D. = C

9. (*a*) Aluminium   (*j*) Manganese
(*b*) Bismuth   (*k*) Platinum
(*c*) Calcium   (*l*) Zinc
(*d*) Helium   (*m*) Silver
(*e*) Neon   (*n*) Gold
(*f*) Radium   (*o*) Copper
(*g*) Chlorine   (*p*) Iron
(*h*) Chromium   (*q*) Sodium
(*i*) Magnesium   (*r*) Lead

Page 46

9. (a) The second sentence means that no pupils may use the pool.
The first sentence means that those pupils who are not good swimmers may not use the pool.

(b) The first sentence means that the dangerous drivers are those who drink too much.
The second sentence means that all drivers drink too much and are a menace.

Page 47

6. (e) MEN'S HAIRDRESSER

Page 48

5. (b) Did you watch 'Grandstand' yesterday?

(d) Don't put 'Local' at the end of the address.

Page 49   SUGGESTED ANSWERS

9. (a) Laverne asked Dione who had taught her to swim.

(b) Dione replied that she had taught herself.

(c) Laverne enquired whether Dione could dive.

(d) Dione said that she could dive off the edge of the bath but not from the springboard.

(e) Laverne exclaimed that Dione should have a go, that it was easy and that there was nothing to be afraid of.

Page 51

4. (g) A swimming-pool.

Page 54

38. minuscule

Page 59

1. mathematics, cookery, needle-work, woodwork, geography, history, typewriting, scripture.

9. an idyllic island

Page 67

61.(e) megalith

62.(c) asterisks

Page 75

8. (b) Flat-fish, e.g., plaice and sole, are caught in trawl-nets.

(c) Kerosene i.e., paraffin is obtained from petroleum.

Page 79

(32) These notes should have been *written* in ink.

Page 84   93.

(b) (i) Parveen lets the grass grow under her feet.
(ii) Fatima puts her best foot forward.

(e) (i) Nurendra found it plain sailing.

Page 86   97.

(m) The new housing estate has *changed the face of* the district.

Page 95   118.

3. (a) a b c c b a a b

Page 96

3. (a) 8.7.8.7

(b) 9.8.9.8

(c) 6.6.4.6.6.6.4

Page 99   126.

(a) Mr. and Mrs. N. Singh,
44, Goldfield Road,
TRING,
Herts. HP23 4AZ

(c) Messrs. B. and W. Edeke,
205, Grange Road,
BIRKENHEAD,
Merseyside L41 2PR

GRAMMAR

1. PHRASES AND SENTENCES

1. (a) Phrase
   (b) Sentence
   (c) Phrase
   (d) Sentence
   (e) Phrase
   (f) Sentence
   (g) Sentence
   (h) Phrase
   (i) Sentence
   (j) Sentence

2. SUGGESTED ANSWERS

   (a) A tarpaulin is a sheet of tarred canvas.
   (b) A delta is a river mouth with many outlets.
   (c) An eel is a slippery snake-like fish.
   (d) Borax is a white salt obtained from the earth.
   (e) An oboe is a wooden wind-instrument.
   (f) The sky is the open space above the earth.
   (g) The elbow is the bend of the arm
   (h) Tinfoil is sheet tin as thin as paper.
   (i) A whale is a huge sea-animal.
   (j) Honey is a sweet juice made by bees.
   (k) Pliers are pincers with flat-faced jaws.
   (l) The dinosaur was a great prehistoric reptile.

   F. D. & C. Manual, p. 35

5. (a) She crept into a back seat.
   (b) We held a party.
   (c) He repaired the net.
   (d) There he stood.
   (e) The men ran for safety.
   (f) I go for a swim.

6. (a) Every pupil, without exception, has passed the examination.
   (b) The fox, tired of trying to reach the grapes, walked away in disgust.
   (c) No man, however strong, could move that boulder.
   (d) Jim, hoping to see Santa Claus, kept one eye open.
   (e) Mary, afraid of the thunder and lightning, put her head under the clothes.
   (f) The peasant, hoping to get rich quickly, killed the goose that laid the golden eggs.

7. (a) So that it will keep in line with the higher fares of the big undertakings.
   Or whether that is just talk.
   (b) The week-end driver with the children in the back.
   The young sports-car enthusiast with his girl friend.
   And the pedestrians, the cyclists,

1

and the coach parties who thronged the fly-over bridges.

(c) A lot of money to spend before a yacht is even started.
But not too much.

(d) From the Chancellor of the Exchequer, good news.
And better advice.

(e) Because he has known fame and glory.

2. COMMON NOUNS

1. (a) The spokes of a *wheel*.
(b) The keel of a *ship* (*boat*, etc.).
(c) The pendulum of a *clock*.
(d) The rungs of a *ladder*.
(e) The fuselage of an *aeroplane*.
(f) The kernel of a *nut*.
(g) The jamb of a *doorway* (*window*, etc.).
(h) The radius of a *circle*, etc.
(i) The pistil of a *flower*.
(j) The estuary of a *river*.

PAGE 3

2. (a) A cello is an *instrument*.
(b) A lizard is a *reptile*.
(c) An antelope is an *animal*.
(d) Spinach is a *vegetable*.
(e) An aster is a *flower*.
(f) A quail is a *bird*.
(g) Granite is a *rock*.
(h) A pomegranate is a *fruit*.
(i) A doublet is a *garment*.
(j) Badminton is a *game*.

3. SUGGESTED ANSWERS

(a) **dynamo.** A <u>machine</u> for making <u>electricity.</u>

(b) **bucket.** A <u>container</u> for carrying <u>water.</u>
(c) **pincers.** A <u>tool</u> for gripping <u>nails.</u>
(d) **camera.** An <u>instrument</u> for taking <u>photographs.</u>
(e) **putty.** A <u>substance</u> for fixing <u>glass.</u>
(f) **wardrobe.** A <u>cupboard</u> for storing <u>clothes.</u>
(g) **catapult.** A <u>device</u> for flinging <u>stones.</u>
(h) **telegraph.** An <u>instrument</u> for sending <u>messages.</u>

4. (a) joke (trick, frolic, escapade)
(b) tomb (burial-place)
(c) law (decree, enactment)
(d) breathing
(e) mercury
(f) wizard (magician)
(g) treacle
(h) paraffin (lamp-oil)

5. employer and workman
doctor and patient
king and subject
host and guest
nobleman and retainer
governess and pupil
mayor and alderman
editor and journalist
lawyer and client

7. (a) beggar
(b) competitor
(c) applicant
(d) representative
(e) student
(f) correspondent
(g) conspirator
(h) braggart
(i) deputy
(j) critic
(k) saviour
(l) dependant

PAGE 4

8. margin, ditch, feet, cauldron, fire, attitude, sound, movements, ruins,

2

man, spoon, hand, horn, dagger, belt, singer, step, lumber, ear, cloak, butterfly, face.

3. PROPER NOUNS

I.

Common	Proper
collar	Plymouth
female	Schubert
rosette	Congo
earthquake	Columbus
telephone	Anne
plumber	Charles
hydrant	Asia
mushroom	Kent
pirate	Venus
conundrum	Easter

3. (a) The name of her school is St. Mary's High School.

(b) The fine earthenware called china is so named because it was brought into Europe from China.

(c) The Hotel Royal is the only hotel I can recommend.

(d) The main gate of the park is at the end of Park Road.

(e) The canary is a song-bird that originated in the Canary Islands.

(f) Merton College is the oldest college in Oxford.

(g) The Black Forest is one of the most beautiful forests in Europe.

(h) It was in 1922 that broadcasting was begun by the British Broadcasting Company.

(i) In 'The Merchant of Venice' he took the part of Antonio the merchant.

(j) North of County Durham is the county of Northumberland.

F. D. & C. Manual, p. 31

4. Pearson, Atkins, Davies, Taylor, Lloyd, Dixon, Carr, Clarke, Knott, Coates, Gay.

5. (a) jersey (e) guillotine
(b) sandwich (f) port
(c) dahlia (g) cambric
(d) worsted (h) volcano

4. VERBS

I. SUGGESTED ANSWERS

(a) Mountaineers *climb.*

(b) Vegetables *grow.*

(c) Fuels *burn.*

(d) Choristers *sing.*

(e) Bees *sting.*

(f) Farmers *plough.*

(g) Water *flows.*

(h) Ice *melts.*

(i) Cork *floats.*

(j) Dynamite *explodes.*

(k) Elastic *stretches.*

(l) Iron *rusts.*

(m) Diamonds *sparkle.*

(n) Authors *write.*

(o) Reptiles *crawl.*

(p) Rodents *gnaw.*

(q) Petrol *evaporates.*

(r) Orators *speak.*

2. SUGGESTED ANSWERS

(a) **plumber.** A man who <u>fits</u> lead pipes, etc.

(b) **milkmaid.** A girl who <u>milks</u> cows.

(c) **sentinel.** A soldier who <u>keeps</u> guard.

(d) **landlord.** A man who <u>owns</u> a rented house, etc.

(e) **sorcerer.** A man who <u>practises</u> magic.

3

(f) **nun.** A woman who <u>leads</u> a religious life in a convent.

(g) **authoress.** A woman who <u>writes</u> books, etc.

(h) **aviator.** A man who <u>flies</u> in aircraft.

3. (a) The little dog <u>laughed</u>.
   (b) The last straw <u>breaks</u> the camel's back.
   (c) The mouse <u>ran</u> up the clock.
   (d) Good King Wenceslas <u>looked</u> out.
   (e) <u>Drink</u> this medicine.
   (f) They <u>fought</u> the dogs, and <u>killed</u> the cats, And <u>bit</u> the babies in the cradles.
   (g) A peck of pickled peppercorns Peter Piper <u>picked</u>.
   (h) Up you <u>go</u>!

4. (a) The producer told me to *shamble* like an old man.
   (b) We shall have to *economize*.
   (c) The vessel began to *wallow* in the waves.
   (d) She is going to Bournemouth to *recuperate*.
   (e) We heard the noise *reverberate* among the cliffs.
   (f) We saw him *grimace* as though he had felt a sharp pain.
   (g) He *masqueraded* as a woman.
   (h) The bandits went out to *waylay* the mail coach.

PAGE 6

5. (a) am   (d) were   (g) grew
   (b) are   (e) was   (h) turned
   (c) is   (f) becomes   (i) get

6. The words to be used in sentences are given here in brackets.

(a) Why did you .... ? (*hesitate*)
(b) At what time .... ? (*begin*)
(c) When the books arrive .... (*arrange*)
(d) I shall need a screwdriver .... (*connect*)
(e) A gang of men arrived .... (*dismantle*)
(f) The reason why I .... (*detest*)
(g) If you speak to Fred like that .... (*provoke*)

7. (a) I <u>wander'd</u> lonely as a cloud.
   (b) The mirror <u>cracked</u> from side to side.
   (c) The ploughman homeward <u>plods</u> his weary way.
   (d) <u>Buy</u> my English posies!
   (e) Like a yawn of fire from the grass it <u>came.</u>
   (f) Now the great winds shoreward <u>blow.</u>
   (g) How solitary <u>gleams</u> the lamplit street.
   (h) The North wind <u>powders</u> me with snow.
   (i) But in the purple pool there nothing <u>grows</u>.
   (j) <u>Blow, blow,</u> thou winter wind.

8. SUGGESTED SYNONYMS

(a) flourished, waved
(b) surrounded, encompassed, besieged
(c) strengthened
(d) threatened
(e) damaged, weakened, injured, harmed
(f) refuse, reject
(g) praise, compliment
(h) fed, grazed
(i) ground
(j) surrendered, submitted, yielded

4

9. (a) to explain   (f) to notify
   (b) to admire   (g) to pronounce
   (c) to recognize   (h) to suspend
   (d) to subscribe   (i) to permit
   (e) to divide   (j) to acquire

PAGE 7

Noun or Verb? (Illustrated exercise)

(1) to box (verb); a box (noun)
(2) to rock (verb); a rock (noun)
(3) to bear (verb); a bear (noun)
(4) a grate (noun); to grate (verb)

5. ONE WORD, TWO USES

1. (a) noun   (g) noun
  (b) verb   (h) verb
  (c) verb   (i) verb
  (d) noun   (j) noun
  (e) verb   (k) noun
  (f) noun   (l) verb

2. (a) noun   (e) noun
  (b) verb   (f) verb
  (c) verb   (g) noun
  (d) noun   (h) noun

PAGE 8

6. SUBJECT AND PREDICATE

1. (a) Peter | <u>drove</u> the car.
  (b) Wax | <u>melts</u> easily.
  (c) Birds of a feather | <u>flock</u> together.
  (d) This motor | <u>works</u> by electricity.
  (e) Thousands of people | <u>perished</u>.
  (f) Mr. Jones, the insurance collector, | <u>called</u> today.

(g) Two large trees | <u>were obstructing</u> the line.
(h) He | <u>is waiting</u> for Trevor.

4. (a) a leopard
  (b) a blue ribbon
  (c) a narrow cart-track
  (d) the bodies of two crusaders
  (e) the news
  (f) the climbers
  (g) the milkman

PAGE 9

6. (a) *A flag* hung from the window.
  (b) *A ditch* lies behind the bushes.
  (c) *A fire* burned brightly in the grate.
  (d) *A policeman* stands at the cross-roads.
  (e) *She* cuts and binds the grain alone.
  (f) *Their knell* is rung by fairy hands.
  (g) *She* went all alone.
  (h) *The great god Pan* sat high on the shore.
  (i) *I* saw ten thousand at a glance.
  (j) *The sound of the far-off bell* swung down.

7. (a) Out of his pocket jumped *a mouse*.
  (b) On each side of him stood *a policeman*.
  (c) Into the street stepped *the Pied Piper*.
  (d) Beyond the town lies *open country*.
  (e) In this dungeon were kept *fifty prisoners*.
  (f) At the head of the stairs stood *two statues*.
  (g) Around the trunk of the tree were tied *thick ropes*.
  (h) Around the bay roared *ragged breakers*.
  (i) Out of the car stepped *the princess*.
  (j) Out rang *the wedding bells*.

7. SINGULAR AND PLURAL

F. D. & C. Manual, p. 48

I. (a) Many wolves
    (b) Various keys
    (c) A few giraffes
    (d) Crowds of women
    (e) Some flies
    (f) Numerous mosquitoes (or mosquitos)

2. | | |
    |---|---|
    | pianos | potatoes |
    | photos | echoes |
    | dynamos | heroes |
    | curios | volcanoes |
    | sopranos | tomatoes |

3. pennies   valleys   pulleys   rubies
    remedies   donkeys   stories   storeys
    journeys   pastries   melodies   kidneys
    The letter before each remaining y is **e**.
    Rule: (i) If the letter before y is a consonant, change the y to i and add **es**.
    (ii) If the letter before y is a vowel, add **s**.

4. SUGGESTED ANSWERS

    bream, cannon, carp, chub, cod, dace, deer, grayling, grouse, gudgeon, haddock, hake, halibut, mackerel, perch, pike, plaice, roach, salmon, sheep, swine, tench, trout, turbot.

5. | | |
    |---|---|
    | (a) A toe | (h) A mackerel |
    | (b) A domino | (i) A child |
    | (c) A wolf | (j) An ox |
    | (d) A cave | (k) A bus |
    | (e) A lady | (l) A man-servant |
    | (f) A pig-sty | (m) A radius |
    | (g) An alley | (n) A cherub |

6. Two teaspoonfuls of medicine
    Three pocketfuls of conkers
    Four basinfuls of broth
    Five wineglassfuls of sherry
    Six bowlfuls of water
    Seven bagfuls of waste paper
    Eight jugfuls of milk
    Nine basketfuls of apples
    Ten shovelfuls of sand
    Eleven bucketfuls of coal
    Twelve handfuls of nuts

7. | | |
    |---|---|
    | (a) bellows | (g) tongs |
    | (b) pincers | (h) trousers |
    | (c) pliers | (i) measles |
    | (d) scissors | (j) mumps |
    | (e) shears | (k) oats |
    | (f) tweezers | (l) soap-suds |

8. (a) The *buses are* late.
    (b) My *sisters-in-law have* returned.
    (c) The *deer were* caught alive.
    (d) The *geese are* ready for market.
    (e) The *mongooses have* killed two snakes.
    (f) *Were* the *armies* defeated?
    (g) *Are* the *kangaroos* fully grown?
    (h) *Have* your *teeth* stopped aching?

9. | *Singular* | *Plural* |
    |---|---|
    | lens | gladioli |
    | terminus | strata |
    | topaz | fungi |
    | aphis | larvae |
    | bureau | plateaux |
    | axis | dice |

    F. D. & C. Manual, pp. 33–34

Singular and Plural (Illustrated exercise)

(1) volcano	(2) baby
volcanoes	babies

6

(3) horse	(8) oasis
horses	oases
(4) piano	(9) handkerchief
pianos	handkerchiefs
(5) mouse	(10) brush
mice	brushes
(6) sheep	(11) loaf, knife
sheep	loaves, knives
(7) chimney	(12) fungus
chimneys	fungi

PAGE 12

8. COLLECTIVE NOUNS

1. (a) A pack of wolves
   (b) A gang of thieves
   (c) A flock of sheep
   (d) A herd of buffaloes
   (e) A litter of puppies
   (f) A horde of savages
   (g) A fusillade (or volley) of rifle-shots
   (h) A batch of loaves
   (i) A school of porpoises
   (j) A covey of partridges
   (k) A flight of stairs
   (l) An anthology of poems

2. (a) manning a ship or boat
   (b) playing musical instruments
   (c) singing, speaking, or dancing together
   (d) listening to a concert or speech, etc.
   (e) waiting for admission or to be served
   (f) dancing, acting, or performing tricks
   (g) worshipping in church
   (h) crowding noisily and angrily in the streets

3.
One kind	*Several kinds*
menagerie	bundle

One kind	*Several kinds*
congregation	flock
forest	herd
orchestra	team
archipelago	gang
bouquet	band
constellation	swarm

[The division given above is debatable, but the words on the left are so grouped because they refer specifically to captive animals, worshippers, trees, instrumentalists, islands, flowers, and stars respectively. Those on the right are usually qualified (e.g., *gang of safe-breakers*, etc.) On the other hand, one may also speak of *a bouquet of roses, a forest of oak-trees*, etc.]

4. (a) Any three of the following:
      assembly, association, band, body, crowd, gathering, group, knot, meeting, mob, multitude, party, queue, throng, tribe.
   (b) Any three of the following:
      army, body, company, corps, platoon, regiment, squad, troop.
   (c) Any three of the following:
      clump, forest, grove, spinney.
   (d) bouquet, bunch, nosegay.
   (e) cluster, constellation, galaxy.

PAGE 13

Plural and Collective (Illustrated exercise)

(1) grapes	(6) hounds
bunch	pack
(2) birds	(7) arrows
flock	sheaf
(3) chickens	(8) eggs
brood	clutch
(4) fish	(9) ships
shoal	fleet or convoy
(5) bees	(10) angels
swarm	host

7

(11) cubs (12) oxen
litter team

PAGE 14

Nouns often confused (Illustrated exercise)

(1) boy; buoy   (4) aisle; isle
(2) leek; leak   (5) quay; key
(3) mare; mayor

PAGE 15

★ REVISION

1. (a) Any ten of the following:
   night, period, roof, world, stars,
   dews, perfumes, hours, changes,
   face, kind, death.
   (b) Nature, Milky Way, Modestine.
   (c) meadows, sheep, hill-sides, ferns,
   men, fowls, eyes.

2. (a) noun   (d) noun
   (b) noun   (e) noun
   (c) verb   (f) verb

3. (a) My tin (or *tin*)
   (b) The black fir-points (or *fir-points*)
   (c) I

4. I could see Modestine walking. I
   could hear her munching. There was
   not another sound.

5. (a) phrase   (d) phrase
   (b) sentence   (e) phrase
   (c) sentence

6. The only essential capital letters are as
   follows:
   To fry ..... You must ..... When

they are fried ..... Squeeze in some
juice .....

Noun or Verb? (Illustrated exercise)

(1) a pound (noun); to pound (verb)
(2) to till (verb); a till (noun)
(3) to swallow (verb); a swallow (noun)
(4) to pelt (verb); a pelt (noun)

PAGE 16

9. ADJECTIVES

1. (a) *Malayan* rubber
   (b) The *Swiss* Alps
   (c) *Norwegian* fiords
   (d) The *Belgian* railways
   (e) A *Dutch* village
   (f) *Brazilian* coffee
   (g) The *Spanish* Civil War
   (h) *Portuguese* history
   (i) *Polish* architecture
   (j) *Mexican* oil
   (k) *Moroccan* tribesmen
   (l) The *Maltese* language
   (m) *Peruvian* cotton
   (n) *Cingalese* customs

2. SUGGESTED ANSWERS

   (a) **tusk.** A <u>long pointed</u> tooth.
   (b) **pebble.** A <u>small round</u> stone.
   (c) **emerald.** A <u>green precious</u> stone.
   (d) **gauze.** <u>Thin transparent</u> cloth.
   (e) **mud.** <u>Soft wet</u> earth.
   (f) **minuet.** A <u>slow, graceful</u> dance.
   (g) **silver.** A <u>precious white</u> metal.
   (h) **banjo.** A <u>stringed musical</u> instru-
       ment.

3. (a) agonizing   (d) infuriated
   (b) exquisite   (e) luscious
   (c) immense   (f) incomparable

8

4. (a) reckless   (e) brusque
   (b) meagre   (f) colossal
   (c) destitute   (g) infirm
   (d) indolent   (h) momentous

5. (a) oily   (g) heavy, iron
   (b) tall, tapering   (h) pink, pale
   (c) cold, untidy,   (i) square, round
   dismal
   (d) stupid, unkind   (j) home-cured,
   (e) brightest   new, garden
   (f) bigger

PAGE 17

7. The following list suggests one of the many possible ways of using twenty alternatives for the word *nice*, without repetition.

   (a) A *luscious* pear
   (b) A *courteous* man
   (c) A *charming* woman
   (d) A *melodious* tune
   (e) A *comfortable* armchair
   (f) A *gorgeous* sunset
   (g) *Excellent* handwriting
   (h) A *beautiful* garden
   (i) A *pretty* frock
   (j) A *jolly* party
   (k) A *tasty* meal
   (l) *Polite* manners
   (m) A *fragrant* smell
   (n) A *magnificent* cathedral
   (o) A *graceful* dance
   (p) An *accomplished* pianist
   (q) A *friendly* neighbour
   (r) A *delightful* gift
   (s) *Pleasant* weather
   (t) A *fine* cat

8. SUGGESTED ANSWERS

   (a) reckless
   (b) enraged, angry, irate, infuriated
   (c) brilliant
   (d) resounding
   (e) magnificent, gorgeous, majestic, superb
   (f) broken-hearted, woebegone
   (g) microscopic, minute
   (h) violent, fierce, furious, raging, wild
   (i) terrified, panic-stricken

9. SUGGESTED ANSWERS

   (a) dirty, soiled, stained
   (b) intelligent, quick-witted, sharp, bright
   (c) foolish, absurd, ridiculous, senseless, silly, stupid
   (d) big, large
   (e) small, little, tiny
   (f) long, lengthy
   (g) old, antiquated, old-fashioned
   (h) discourteous, rude, ill-mannered, ungentlemanly
   (i) untidy, shabby, slovenly, unkempt
   (j) valuable, excellent, first-rate
   (k) ugly, unshapely, unsightly
   (l) painful, unpleasant, annoying, disagreeable

10. SUGGESTED ANSWERS

   (a) *Untruthful* men (or *deceitful*)
   (b) A *cowardly* soldier (or *timid*, *chicken-hearted*)
   (c) *Old-fashioned* tools (or *ancient*, *primitive, prehistoric*)
   (d) *Clumsy* fingers (or *awkward, fumbling*)
   (e) An *unselfish* person (or *generous*, *open-handed*)
   (f) A *near* relation (or *close*)
   (g) People who are *poor* (or *destitute*, *needy, penniless, poverty-stricken*)
   (h) The *dull* side of the paper (or *mat*)
   (i) An experience that was *unpleasant*

9

(or *disagreeable, painful, distressing, distasteful*)

(*j*) *Insufficient* meat for a week

II. SUGGESTED ANSWERS

(*a*) fierce, cat-like
(*b*) crafty, cunning, reddish-brown
(*c*) horse-like, striped
(*d*) thick-skinned, horned
(*e*) small, furry, domestic
(*f*) huge, extinct
(*g*) rough-haired, thick-furred, large
(*h*) grey-haired, burrowing
(*i*) keen-eyed, sharp-sighted
(*j*) imaginary, fabulous

PAGE 18

I2. SUGGESTED ANSWERS

(*a*) dusty, filthy, soiled, stained
(*b*) choice, excellent, first-rate, exquisite, fine, high-class
(*c*) agile, fast, light-footed, nimble
(*d*) deadly, dreadful, horrible
(*e*) deafening, ear-splitting, resounding, tumultuous
(*f*) indolent, languid, lazy, listless, slothful, sluggish

F. D. & C. Manual, p. 54

I3. (*a*) experimental (*g*) courteous
(*b*) complimentary (*h*) charitable
(*c*) microscopic (*i*) spectacular
(*d*) skilful (*j*) systematic
(*e*) intellectual (*k*) chivalrous
(*f*) metropolitan (*l*) tempestuous

I4. (*a*) scholastic (*g*) burdensome
(*b*) cylindrical (*h*) asthmatic
(*c*) discordant (*i*) argumentative
(*d*) matrimonial (*j*) nutritious
(*e*) negligent (*k*) derisive
(*f*) apathetic (*l*) longitudinal

I5. 1. *Quality*	2. *Quantity*	3. *Demonstrative*
high	six	this
proud	several	these
sharp	few	those
ugly	some	that
clean	all	his
famous	both	my

I6. (*a*) noun (*f*) adjective
(*b*) adjective (*g*) noun
(*c*) adjective (*h*) noun
(*d*) noun (*i*) adjective
(*e*) noun (*j*) noun

PAGE 19

10. COMPOUND WORDS

F. D. & C. Manual, p. 33

I. SUGGESTED ANSWERS

(*a*) rainbow, rainfall
(*b*) firearm, firebrand, firelight, fireman, fireplace, fireside, firewood, firework
(*c*) sunbeam, sunburn, sundial, sunlight, sunstroke, sunspot
(*d*) postcard, postman, postmark, postmaster
(*e*) bedroom, bedstead, bedtime, bedspread, bedrock
(*f*) snowball, snowfall, snowflake, snowstorm
(*g*) seaman, seaport, seashore, seaside, seaweed
(*h*) daybreak, daylight, daytime, daydream
(*i*) football, foothill, foothold, footlights, footman, footpath, footprint, footstep, footstool, footnote, footbridge, footplate

(j) playfellow, playground, playtime, playmate, plaything, playwright

(k) farmhouse, farmyard

(l) bookcase, bookmaker, bookmark, bookseller, bookshelf, bookstall, bookworm

(m) necklace, necktie, neckband, neckcloth, neckwear

(n) roadside, roadway, roadman

(o) buttercup, butterfly, buttermilk

2. SUGGESTED ANSWERS

(a) nightcap, nightdress, nightfall, nightgown, nightshade, nightshirt, nightmare

(b) moonbeam, moonlight, moonshine, moonstone

(c) watercourse, waterfall, waterman, watermark, waterspout, waterworks

(d) lifebelt, lifeboat, lifebuoy, lifeline, lifetime

(e) skylark, skylight, skyline

(f) aircraft, airman, airport, airship

(g) landlady, landlord, landmark, landowner, landslide

(h) hedgehog, hedgerow

(i) housebreaker, householder, housekeeper, housemaid, housetop, housewife

(j) backache, backbone, background, backwash, backwater, backwoods

(k) staircase, stairway

(l) eyeball, eyebrow, eyeglass, eyelash, eyewash

3. SUGGESTED ANSWERS

(a) coachman, dustman, policeman, quarryman

(b) earthwork, ironwork, needlework, stonework

(c) lighthouse, playhouse, warehouse, workhouse

(d) candlelight, gaslight, lamplight, torchlight

(e) hearthstone, ironstone, millstone, sandstone

(f) butterfly, dragonfly, firefly, mayfly

(g) bellflower, cornflower, sunflower, wallflower

(h) crowberry, dogberry, snowberry, strawberry

(i) churchyard, courtyard, dockyard, shipyard

(j) bedside, countryside, riverside, wayside

4. (Illustrated exercise)

(1) headlight or headlamp; headland; headline; headstone

(2) handbag; handrail; handcuffs; handkerchief

(3) woodcutter, woodman, or woodland; woodpecker; woodcock; woodbine

5.
(a) chicken-hearted
(b) eagle-eyed
(c) open-handed
(d) tight-fisted
(e) hare-brained
(f) stiff-necked
(g) light-fingered
(h) thick-skinned
(i) weak-kneed
(j) hard-headed

PAGE 20

6.
(a) hair-raising		(g) hang-dog	
(b) red-letter		(h) gilt-edged	
(c) rock-bottom		(i) time-honoured	
(d) deep-seated		(j) heart-rending	
(e) hard-earned		(k) long-standing	
(f) cold-blooded		(l) high-flown	

11

11. GENDER

1. stallion   buck   nephew   duke
   master   lad   wizard   he-goat
   boar   sir   monk   manservant

2. countess   filly   mayoress   hostess
   sultana   spinster   ewe   tabby-cat

3.
Masculine	Feminine
drake	pullet
gander	heifer
heir	tabby-cat
Jew	ewe
peer	filly
blond	belle

Common	Neuter
singer	cloud
puppy	vase
passenger	window
player	ship
assistant	moon
spectator	tulip

A *ship* and the *moon* may be referred to as *she*.

4. Of the large number of acceptable answers the following are a representative selection.

teacher	speaker	visitor
candidate	contributor	saint
competitor	employee	hypocrite
climber	client	dependant
winner	owner	monarch
pianist	resident	scholar
dancer	worshipper	expert
subscriber	liar	cyclist
employer	child	performer
shopkeeper	pessimist	instrumentalist
tenant	student	artist

inhabitant	novice	correspondent
lover	swimmer	sympathizer
thief	motorist	customer
infant	vocalist	seller
optimist	chorister	official
pupil	writer	partner
absentee	critic	sinner
runner	agent	snob
athlete	buyer	slave
loser	applicant	councillor
violinist		

5. SUGGESTED ANSWERS

   authoress, baroness, deaconess, heiress, hostess, Jewess, lioness, manageress, mayoress, peeress, poetess, priestess, prophetess, shepherdess, stewardess, tailoress.

6. SUGGESTED ANSWERS

   abbess, actress, conductress, duchess, empress, enchantress, goddess, governess, huntress, instructress, marchioness, murderess, Negress, princess, proprietress, sorceress, traitress, waitress.

PAGE 21

7. (Illustrated exercise)
   (1) bridegroom   bride
   (2) negro   negress
   (3) actor   actress
   (4) peacock   peahen
   (5) brave   squaw
   (6) stag or hart   hind

8. The following, in the masculine form only, are given as an indication of the many possible answers:

bachelor	brother	cockerel	earl
boar	buck	colt	father
boy	bull	dog	fox
brave	cock	drake	gander

12

gentleman	man	sire	stallion
hart	monk	sloven	uncle
king	nephew	son	wizard
lord	ram	stag	

9. (a) conductor, conductress
   (b) instructor, instructress
   (c) hunter, huntress
   (d) manager, manageress
   (e) prophet, prophetess
   (f) abbot, abbess
   (g) landlord, landlady
   (h) sorcerer, sorceress
   (i) waiter, waitress
   (j) hero, heroine
   (k) emperor, empress

10. pencil, *neuter*   pen, *neuter*
    lady, *f.*   bridge, *neuter*
    doctor, *common*   door, *neuter*
    woman, *f.*   meadow, *neuter*
    flower, *neuter*   fox, *m.*
    sea, *neuter*   witch, *f.*
    gentleman, *m.*   bull, *m.*
    sheep, *common*   earth, *neuter*
    person, *common*   victim, *common*
        wine, *neuter*

Related words in English:

crayon; dame, dam, damsel; female, feminine; fleuret; mat(t)ins, matinée, matutinal; mere, mermaid; Messrs.; mutton; plume (feather), plumage; pontoon; port, portal, portcullis; portico; Reynard; sorcerer; taurine, toreador; terrace, terrain, terrestrial, territory; vine, vineyard, vintage, vintner, vinegar.

Words of the same gender in both languages:

lady, woman, gentleman, fox, witch, bull.

12. TENSE

1. (a) present   (d) present
   (b) past   (e) present
   (c) past   (f) past

2. (a) .... she *played* the piano.
   (b) .... we *spoke* softly.
   (c) .... I *was* very happy.
   (d) .... the snow *fell* thickly.
   (e) .... children *fed* the swans.

3. (a) .... they *wear* scarves.
   (b) .... I *have* no money.
   (c) .... Jill *goes* up the hill.
   (d) .... she *sells* sea-shells on the sea-shore.
   (e) .... Jack Horner *eats* his pudding.

4. SUGGESTED ANSWERS
   (a) TRAWLER SINKS IN CHANNEL
   (b) OFFICER LOSES SECRET DOCUMENT
   (c) GANG STEALS £15,000
   (d) BROTHERS FALL FROM SCAFFOLD
   (e) ENGINE PLUNGES DOWN EMBANKMENT
   (f) LIGHTNING STRIKES STEEPLE
   (g) EARTHQUAKE SHAKES ATHENS
   (h) BEES STING CITY SHOPPERS

5. (a) was cracked; *past tense*
   (b) shall go; *future tense*
   (c) will help; *future tense*
   (d) are eating; *present tense*
   (e) shall bring; *future tense*
   (f) is working; *present tense*

7. (a) The wheel <u>runs</u> on ball bearings.
   (*Present*)

13

(b) George <u>will tell</u> you the way. (*Future*)

(c) The walls and shelves <u>are</u> grey. (*Present*)

(d) Crinolines <u>were</u> fashionable in those days. (*Past*)

(e) Father <u>will go</u> with me to the station. (*Future*)

(f) I <u>eat</u> my food too quickly. (*Present*)

(g) We <u>shall swim</u> in the river. (*Future*)

(h) The Vicar <u>read</u> the first lesson. (*Past*)

(i) One of these stamps <u>cost</u> ten pence. (*Past*)

(j) I <u>expect</u> a snowstorm. (*Present*)

8. Past tense, present tense, and future tense follow each other in this order.

9. The place *was* extremely black and dirty, and the people *were* rough and uneducated. The men *earned* a good deal of money, but they *spent* it upon eating and drinking. On Saturday the market *was* one of the noisiest exhibitions imaginable, and the so-called amusement of bull-baiting still *existed*. There *were* no schools; the children *played* in the streets from the time that they *could* run till they *went* to the factory, and there they *worked* till they *had* children themselves to do the same thing again.

10. The mixed trains *consisted* of both first-class and second-class coaches; the latter *had* no cushions, or divisions of the compartments. Both kinds *had* seats on the roof for the accommodation of those who *preferred* riding outside. Each passenger's luggage *was* placed on the roof of the coach in which he *took* his place; carpet bags *went* underneath the seat opposite that which the owner *occupied*.

Every train *was* provided with Guards, and a Conductor, who *was* responsible for the order and regularity of the journey. No smoking *was* allowed in the Station-houses, or in any of the coaches, even with the consent of the passengers.

Trains *ran* from Birmingham to Liverpool twice daily, and the journey *took* a little over five hours.

11. I *push* open the door and *go* inside. The house *is* in darkness. Upstairs a door *creaks*. I *stand* stock still, but silence *falls* again. I *take* out a match and *strike* it, but before I *can* light the candle a gust of wind from the doorway *blows* out the flame. In the grounds an owl *hoots*. A shiver *runs* down my spine, and I *can* neither move nor speak.

12. The verbs are given here as alternatives, thus: *past/present*.

We *saw/see* a light shining at the foot of the cliff, so we *picked/pick* our way down the narrow path towards it. Brambles *scratched/scratch* our legs, and our feet *slipped/slip* on the wet clay. A stiff breeze that *blew/blows* from the sea *carried/carries* salt spray to our lips, and *brought/brings* to our ears the sound of rowlocks. There *was/is* no moon, but in the last remnant of twilight we *could/can* see figures moving on the beach, though we *could/can* not make out who they *were/are*. Determined to find out what *was/is* going on we *quickened/quicken* our pace, hoping that we *should/shall* not be heard.

14

13. ABSTRACT NOUNS

1. (a) A hero is praised for his *heroism*.
   (b) A friend is valued for his *friendship*.
   (c) A child goes to school during his *childhood*.
   (d) A slave has to endure *slavery*.
   (e) A tyrant is hated for his *tyranny*.
   (f) A robber is arrested for *robbery*.
   (g) An infant has to be nursed during its *infancy*.
   (h) A coward is despised for his *cowardice*.

2. (a) A kind person pleases others by his *kindness*.
   (b) A skilful acrobat displays his *skill*.
   (c) An active volcano shows signs of *activity*.
   (d) A famous man is one who has achieved *fame*.
   (e) A determined pupil works with *determination*.
   (f) A generous person is noted for his *generosity*.
   (g) An elegant woman is admired for her *elegance*.
   (h) A stupid person should be pitied for his *stupidity*.

   F. D. & C. Manual, p. 23

3. (a) To hate a person is to show *hatred*.
   (b) To free a prisoner is to give him his *freedom*.
   (c) To grieve is to experience a feeling of *grief*.
   (d) To please one's mother is to give her *pleasure*.
   (e) To satisfy one's teachers is to give them *satisfaction*.

(f) To encourage a boy is to give him *encouragement*.
(g) To exaggerate is to be guilty of *exaggeration*.
(h) To deceive people is to practise *deceit*.

4. jealous   friendly   courageous proud
   wise   insolent   poor   hopeful
   vain   humble   heroic   envious
   patriotic grateful

5. (a) insolence   (l) penitence
   (b) flattery   (m) petulance
   (c) prudence   (n) leniency
   (d) fidelity   (o) jubilation
   (e) vigilance   (p) servility
   (f) tolerance   (q) vulgarity
   (g) sagacity   (r) modesty
   (h) animosity   (s) optimism
   (i) candour   (t) temperance
   (j) vivacity   (u) discretion
   (k) pessimism

14. CONJUNCTIONS

1. (a) The walnut was brought into Britain by the Romans, *but* its original home was Persia.
   (b) The beech is a magnificent tree with a massive trunk, *and* its timber is very useful for many purposes.
   (c) The branches of the oak twist about in zig-zag fashion, *and* the thick bark is deeply furrowed.
   (d) In towns the lime is usually a stunted tree, *but* in the country it rivals even the elm in appearance.
   (e) In winter the hornbeam can be

15

mistaken for the beech, *but* it is far less picturesque.

(f) The long trunk of the elm usually has one or two large horizontal limbs, *and* the corky bark is very rugged.

(g) We think of conifers as evergreen trees, *but* the larch loses its leaves in winter.

(h) The osier can be found on river-banks, *and* it can generally be recognized by its long and upward-thrusting branches.

2. SUGGESTED ANSWERS

(a) The sun came out *and* the birds sang again.

(b) There are thousands of bees in the hive, *but* only the queen lays eggs.

(c) Penguins cannot fly, *although* they have wings.

(d) Will you have tea, *or* do you prefer coffee?

(e) The wind became stronger, *so* the captain decided to seek shelter.

(f) The tower is called the Eiffel Tower *because* a man named Eiffel designed it.

(g) The nurse bandaged my leg *after* the doctor had stitched the wound.

(h) The electricity was cut off *while* mother was cooking the dinner.

(i) The story is a strange one, *yet* it is true.

(j) I cannot help you, *though* I should very much like to do so.

F. D. & C. Manual, p. 34

3. SUGGESTED ANSWERS

(a) The lighthouse-keepers cannot be relieved *because* heavy seas are still breaking over the rock.

(b) After covering half the course he was still walking strongly, *although* his feet were badly blistered.

(c) The ice suddenly closed in *and* the ship became jammed between two floes.

(d) Thieves stole luggage and clothing from his car *while* he was calling on friends near by.

(e) The mouse kept on nibbling at the net *until* at last the lion was able to escape.

(f) More than ten thousand people attended the show, *but* the organizers are doubtful whether the event will make a profit.

PAGE 26

4. (a) They were late for school *because* the bus broke down.
Because the bus broke down they were late for school.

(b) She writes beautifully *although* she is blind.
Although she is blind she writes beautifully.

(c) Mary cut the bread and butter *while* Joy was making the tea.
While Joy was making the tea, Mary cut the bread and butter.

(d) They huddled closer together *as* the night grew colder.
As the night grew colder they huddled closer together.

(e) I replaced the shoes on the shelf *after* I had cleaned them.
After I had cleaned them I replaced the shoes on the shelf.

(f) Paper is cheap *because* it is plentiful.
Because it is plentiful, paper is cheap.

16

Alternative answers in Question 2:

(c) *Although* they have wings, penguins cannot fly.

(f) *Because* a man named Eiffel designed it, the tower is called the Eiffel Tower.

(g) *After* the doctor had stitched the wound, the nurse bandaged my leg.

(h) *While* Mother was cooking the dinner, the electricity was cut off.

5. SUGGESTED ANSWERS

(a) *As* the cowboy rode round the ring, two clowns were trying to lasso him, *but* he galloped away without being caught.

(b) *When* the piston reaches the top of the cylinder a spark fires the mixture of air and petrol-vapour, *and* the piston is forced downwards again.

(c) *After* the king had been killed in battle there was a long period of strife and unrest, *until* the young prince was old enough to ascend the throne.

(d) *Because* the rudder was jammed, the boat went round in circles, *so* the captain was compelled to stop the engines.

(e) *As* the sun rose inch by inch above the horizon, slender tongues of flame began to reach across the fields, *until* at last the whole valley was aglow with the morning light.

PAGE 27

15. THE OBJECT

1. (a) The rocket [hit] the moon.

(b) The geese [chased] us.

(c) Mr. Deakin [keeps] cocker spaniels.

(d) A fierce gale [uprooted] many trees.

(e) The gipsies [made] pegs and baskets.

(f) During the holiday I [read] Heidi.

(g) In four matches he [scored] five hundred runs.

(h) Robert [caught] , without any help, a large salmon.

2. (a) Brian [cut] his finger with a chisel.

(b) Mother [called] me at eight o'clock.

(c) I [sold] my stamp album for fifty pence.

(d) A thousand people [lost] their homes in the flood.

(e) Stanford, with the greatest ease, [turned] the ball past Hollins for a single.

(f) Yesterday we [met] uncle in the park.

(g) In the fork of the tree the boys [built] a small hut as an observation post.

3. (a) started (I)   (c) spilt (T)
   (b) sold (T)   (d) melts (I)

17

(e) scrub (T) (g) set (I)
(f) can borrow (T) (h) were running (I)

4. (a) 1. transitive (d) 1. transitive
   2. intransitive 2. intransitive
   (b) 1. intransitive (e) 1. transitive
   2. transitive 2. intransitive
   (c) 1. intransitive
   2. transitive

5. strive, slink, lie, fall, ebb, die, remain, blossom, consent, appear.

6. purify, encourage, annoy, invite, defeat, amaze, possess, afford, disturb, correct.

7. (a) Please *lay* the table.
   (b) They could not *raise* the slab.
   (c) We saw the foresters *fell* the tree.

8. (a) 1. intransitive (d) 1. transitive
   2. transitive 2. intransitive
   (b) 1. transitive (e) 1. transitive
   2. intransitive 2. intransitive
   (c) 1. intransitive (f) 1. intransitive
   2. transitive 2. transitive

★ REVISION

1. (a) a house that is green; a hothouse for plants.
   (b) a bottle that is blue; a large blue fly.
   (c) a skin that is red; an American Indian.
   (d) a bird that is black; a black songbird of the thrush family.

The words in italics are compound words.

2. (a) I *knew* that he *had* a bicycle.
   (b) I *wrote* to him each week while he *was* away.
   (c) We *sat* and *froze*.
   (d) He *sang* as he *dug*.
   (e) The dog *ran* until he *caught* a hare.
   (f) I *chose* my own books when I *went* there.

3. SUGGESTED ANSWERS
   (a) A spanner is a tool for turning nuts on bolts.
   (b) A gourd is a large fruit with a tough rind.
   (c) A nomad is a member of a wandering tribe.
   (d) Lichen is a kind of moss that grows on tree-trunks, etc.
   (e) A weevil is a small beetle that damages crops.
   (f) Talcum is a smooth soft powder.
   (g) A rodent is a gnawing animal.
   (h) Radium is a rare and precious metal.
   (i) A placard is a poster or large bill.

4. (a) clear, coloured, jewel-like, frosty, faint.
   (b) light, living; slumber.
   (c) Present tense.
   (d) *I* is the subject, and *it* is the object.
   (e) whiteness.
   (f) Cattle *awoke* on the meadows; sheep *broke* their fast on dewy hillsides, and *changed* to a new lair among the ferns; and houseless men, who *had* lain down with the fowls, *opened* their dim eyes and *beheld* the beauty of the night.
   (g) but, and.
   (h) Subject: men. Object: eyes.

18

Nouns often confused (Illustrated exercise)

(1) cymbals; symbols (4) yoke; yolk
(2) cygnet; signet (5) hoard; horde
(3) pier; peer

🕮 LOOK THESE UP

1. pŏt   hōld   mīnd   dĕn
   căp   spāde   dūty   bŭt
   sēnior   dĭp   păck   rīght

2. im-   il-   in-   ir-   un-
   unnatural   immortal
   immovable   ·unnoticed

3. (a) Each word begins with the prefix *un-*. In *unnoticed* the prefix is followed by another letter *n*, whereas in *uncertain* it is followed by *c*.
   (b) Acceptable answers: dissatisfy, dissimilar, disservice; also (less obviously) dissect, dissemble, disseminate, dissent, dissociate, dissolve, dissuade.

4. Because the letter before the *y*, in each word, is a vowel.

5. Because the *l* is preceded by a pair of vowels.

6. Aspirates are aitches that should be sounded, and the taxi-driver had dropped one.

16. PRONOUNS

1. (a) they = Alan and Margaret
     them = some blackberries

(b) he   = Tinker
    him = Tinker

(c) I   = Anne
    you = Roger
    it   = the pullover

(d) we   = Brian and Martin
    she = mother
    us   = Brian and Martin

(e) you = the nurse
    me = father
    her = Sheila Foster

(f) he   = Philip
    her = Jane
    it   = the aquarium
    him = Philip

(g) she = Audrey
    them = Mr. and Mrs. Jackson
    it   = the handbag

(h) we   = Sylvia and Frank
    they = the turkeys
    us   = Sylvia and Frank

2. SUGGESTED IMPROVEMENTS ARE SHOWN IN ITALICS

(a) Whose father has had the accident?
Fred was told about his father's accident by Clive. (Or *vice versa*)

(b) Who was shopping?
While Jill was shopping with her mother she saw Judith. (Or *vice versa*)

(c) Does the question refer to the children or to the rabbits?
1. *Have you seen Carol and Trevor looking for their pet rabbits in the field?*
2. *Have you seen the pet rabbits that Carol and Trevor are looking for in the field?*

19

(*d*) Who is suggested as the new team manager?

> *Stephen suggested to Stuart that it might be a good thing if he (Stuart) took over the duties of team manager.* (Alternatively, put *Stephen* in parenthesis.)

(*e*) It is the camera, in this sentence, that darted back into the wood.

> *Tony reached for his camera to photograph the deer, but before he could pick it up the deer had darted back into the wood.*

(*f*) The trainers, according to this sentence, were dead when they woke in the morning.

> *When the trainers settled down for the night their horses were alive and well, but when they woke in the morning the horses were dead.*

3.

Subject	Object
he	us
she	him
we	her
I	them
they	me

4. (*a*) He met them.   (*g*) They met her.
  (*b*) She met him.   (*h*) They met us.
  (*c*) He met her.   (*i*) She met them.
  (*d*) She met her.   (*j*) We met him.
  (*e*) We met her.   (*k*) She met us.
  (*f*) He met us.   (*l*) We met them.

PAGE 31

5. (*a*) We saw her.   (*d*) He saw her.
  (*b*) He saw them.   (*e*) He saw us.
  (*c*) She saw her.   (*f*) She saw him.

(*g*) She saw them.   (*j*) She saw us.
(*h*) They saw her.   (*k*) They saw us.
(*i*) We saw him.   (*l*) We saw them.

6. (*a*) This pen *is yours.*
  (*b*) These coats *are ours.*
  (*c*) That handbag *is hers.*
  (*d*) This house *is theirs.*
  (*e*) That cricket bag *was mine.*
  (*f*) Two of the dogs *were his.*

7. (*a*) We *ourselves* took a photograph of the Princess.

> We took a photograph of the Princess *herself.*

(*b*) I *myself* will be responsible for buying all the food if you will prepare the meal.

> I will be responsible for buying all the food if you *yourself* will prepare the meal.

(*c*) The train *itself* was badly damaged, but the passengers were not injured.

> The train was badly damaged, but the passengers *themselves* were not injured.

(*d*) Wait until Miss Reeves *herself* returns, and ask her if she is willing to present the prizes.

> Wait until Miss Reeves returns, and ask her if she *herself* is willing to present the prizes.

(*e*) Mr. Arden *himself* composed the music, but he did not take part in the performance.

> Mr. Arden composed the music, but he *himself* did not take part in the performance.

(*f*) He *himself* was anxious to take the girls on the water chute, but they were not willing.

He was anxious to take the girls on the water chute, but they *themselves* were not willing.

8. (a) 1. Third person singular
   2. We washed our hands.
   (b) 1. Second person singular
   2. I am my own master.
   (c) 1. Third person plural
   2. You must learn to stand on your own feet.
   (d) 1. First person singular
   2. We hung our heads in shame.
   (e) 1. Third person singular
   2. They are beautiful valleys.
   (f) 1. Second person plural
   2. We must all remember to bring our raincoats.
   (g) 1. First person singular
   2. They will be glad to be on their own.

9. (a) First person singular
   (b) Third person plural
   (c) Third person singular
   (d) Third person singular
   (e) First person plural
   (f) Third person singular
   (g) Third person plural
   (h) First person plural

11. (a) Miss Anne Derry thanks Mr. and Mrs. L. J. Neville for inviting *her* to *their* son's coming-of-age party, and has much pleasure in accepting.
   (b) The Directors wish all *their* employees the compliments of the season, and hope that *they* will enjoy *their* Christmas holiday.
   (c) Mr. Stanley Lovatt thanks the staff and pupils of Milford School for inviting *him* to *their* annual dance, but regrets that owing to a previous engagement *he* will be unable to attend.
   (d) Mr. and Mrs. L. W. Hayward thank Mrs. Bridgeman for inviting *them* to the wedding of *her* daughter on 10th May, but regret that owing to the fact that they will be abroad at that time *they* are unable to accept.
   (e) James Burton assures *his* customers that they will receive the same attention as in the past, and that *he* will do *his* best to have the rebuilding done before May.
   (f) Mrs. S. B. Palmer wishes *her* friends and neighbours to know how grateful *she* is for the kindness *they* have shown to *her* during *her* recent bereavement.

12.(a) He/She is grateful for the invitation.
   (b) He/She hopes to be present.
   (c) He/She has much pleasure in accepting the invitation.
   (d) He/She will be happy to attend.
   (e) It gives him/her much pleasure to accept.
   (f) He/She regrets that he/she will not be able to attend the party.
   (g) He/She would have liked to be present.

13. SUGGESTED ANSWER

Richard Roe thanks all those electors who voted for him on Tuesday, and is pleased to have the opportunity of representing them on the Council. He will do his utmost to serve the district to the best of his ability, and hopes that he will at all times be worthy of the trust that the electors have placed in him.

14. SUGGESTED ANSWERS

(a) Patients should bring their own soap and towels.

(b) Members are requested to pay their annual subscriptions before 31st January.

(c) Customers should ask the supervisor to help them if they need advice.

(d) Hirers will have their deposits returned to them when they bring back their boats in good condition.

(e) The operator should depress the knob with his thumb, and move the lever away from him until he can push it no farther.

15. (a) Have you found me, O my enemy?

(b) Out of your own mouth will I judge you.

(c) If your eye offends you, pluck it out.

(d) You fool, this night your soul shall be required of you.

(e) When you do alms, let not your left hand know what your right hand does.

17. ADVERBS

1. (a) He played golf *skilfully*.

(b) He answered me *impudently*.

(c) She described her experiences *humorously*.

(d) They proceeded *cautiously*.

(e) The victors marched into the city *triumphantly*.

(f) We were urged to give *generously*.

(g) The appeal was received *charitably*.

(h) She nursed her patients *devotedly*.

(i) He made the model *ingeniously*.

2. (a) The diameter of the wheel was measured *precisely*.

(b) In his speech and actions he behaved *discreetly*.

(c) Mary looked at her broken doll *dejectedly*.

(d) The old man treated the village children *benevolently*.

(e) The birds sang *melodiously*.

(f) He gave his opinion *candidly*.

(g) She blushed, and replied *diffidently*.

(h) The bulldog held on *tenaciously*.

(i) She sewed it *dexterously*.

3. (a) To live *unhappily*

(b) To speak *untruthfully*

(c) To struggle *helplessly*

(d) To work *unskilfully*

(e) To jump *fearlessly*

(f) To act *senselessly*

(g) To talk *unwisely*

(h) To behave *thoughtlessly*

4. (a) To answer *impatiently*

(b) To move *irregularly*

(c) To sew *imperfectly*

(d) To count *incorrectly*

(e) To behave *disloyally*

(f) To measure *inaccurately*

(g) To speak *disrespectfully*

(h) To talk *irreverently*

(a) *For what reason* are you crying?

(b) Hang your coat *in this place*.

(c) I looked for him *in every place*.

(d) It must be *in one place or another*.

(e) You will learn *in a short time*.

(f) Do this exercise *at the present time*.

(g) I go camping *many times*.

(h) She was to be seen *in no place*.

6. SUGGESTED ANSWERS

(a) **scamper.** To run <u>hastily</u>.

(b) **warble.** To sing <u>like a bird</u>.

(c) **smoulder.** To burn <u>slowly without flame.</u>

(d) **scribble.** To write <u>very carelessly</u>.

(e) **prowl.** To roam <u>in search of prey</u>.

(f) **shatter.** To break <u>suddenly into many pieces</u>.

(g) **waddle.** To walk <u>with a rocking movement.</u>

(h) **vibrate.** To move <u>to and fro rapidly.</u>

7. (a) Why are you so *slow*?
Why are you walking so *slowly*?

(b) She fell *heavily*.
The box was *heavy*.

(c) Speak more *distinctly*.
His speech is not very *distinct*.

(d) You chose the *wrong* one.
You have nailed this *wrongly*.

(e) I did it *accidentally*.
It was an *accidental* mistake.

(f) In all his habits he is very *regular*.
He does this *regularly*.

(g) This switch works *differently*.
This switch is *different*.

(h) Be sure to make the gate *secure*.
Be sure to lock the gate *securely*.

8. (a) She walked out *proudly* for her prize.

(b) His voice was loud and *clear*.

(c) She referred *scornfully* to my parents.

(d) Why did he answer me so *angrily*?

(e) Fruit is *plentiful* this year.

(f) Be sure to add these figures *correctly*.

(g) The infants danced ever so *prettily*.

(h) The room had been made clean and *tidy*.

9.
secretly	harshly	similarly
closely	actively	angrily
truthfully	skilfully	nobly
humbly	gently	truly
gaily	fully	wholly

regularly	bravely
busily	clumsily
feebly	gracefully
majestically	frantically
coolly	slyly

10.
Time	Place	Manner
now	here	bravely
immediately	everywhere	silently
soon	anywhere	courteously
then	there	

Number	Degree
twice	violently
occasionally	wholly
repeatedly	slightly
frequently	exceedingly
always	scarcely

F. D. & C. Manual, p. 24

11. SUGGESTED ANSWERS

(a) I was received *courteously*.

(b) He shouted for help *repeatedly*.

(c) He writes to me *occasionally*.
(d) We searched *everywhere*.
(e) I want it done *immediately*.
(f) The car was *slightly* damaged.
(g) They came in *silently*.

12. SUGGESTED ANSWERS

(a) To reply *angrily* (or *scornfully, irately*)
(b) To resist *obstinately* (or *doggedly, resolutely*)
(c) To act *foolishly* (or *absurdly, stupidly, ridiculously*)
(d) To behave *dishonestly* (or *deceitfully, falsely, unfairly*)
(e) To smile *shyly* (or *sheepishly, diffidently*)
(f) To grow *plentifully* (or *prolifically*)
(g) To be furnished *magnificently* (or *richly, lavishly, superbly*)
(h) To stand *prominently* (or *plainly, clearly*)

PAGE 36

13.(a) If a policeman were to *turn up*, those boys would be in trouble.
(b) At nine o'clock we decided to *turn in*.
(c) When the last performance is over, everyone in the circus has to *turn to*.
(d) The way was blocked, so we had to *turn about*.
(e) Why did they *fall out*?
(f) The soldiers were ordered to *fall in*.
(g) I hope our plans do not *fall through*.
(h) If Mr. Charles is ill the concert will have to be *put off*.
(i) The riot was *put down* quickly.
(j) The vicar lost the place in his notes, but was not at all *put out*.

14. SUGGESTED ANSWERS

(a) Our aim is to carry out our customers' orders satisfactorily and efficiently.
(b) I like to go occasionally to a play or to a concert.
(c) Sometimes, if not always, the best plan is to finish off with a window-leather.
(d) To do one's duty conscientiously is better than to be selfishly indulgent.

NOTE. Observations on the split infinitive are to be found in *Modern English Usage* (Fowler), *Usage and Abusage* (Partridge), *ABC of Plain Words* (Gowers), and *ABC of English Usage* (Treble and Vallins). Reference is made in later pages to other debatable constructions discussed in these books.

18. COMPARISON OF ADJECTIVES

F. D. & C. Manual, p. 31

I.

POSITIVE	COMPARATIVE	SUPERLATIVE
long	longer	longest
wet	wetter	wettest
big	bigger	biggest
shiny	shinier	shiniest
sad	sadder	saddest
hot	hotter	hottest
lonely	lonelier	loneliest
thin	thinner	thinnest
slim	slimmer	slimmest
dry	drier	driest
sly	slyer	slyest

2. more dainty,   more fierce,
most angry,   most gloomy,
most clever,   most lovely,
more gentle,   more wise,
most jolly,   most noble,
more wealthy,   more silly.

3.

POSITIVE	COMPARATIVE	SUPERLATIVE
short	shorter	shortest
noisy	noisier	noisiest
important	more important	most important
peaceful	more peaceful	most peaceful
shabby	shabbier	shabbiest
good	better	best
shy	shyer	shyest
far	farther	farthest
old	elder	eldest
bad	worse	worst
much	more	most
little	less	least

PAGE 37

4. (a) The *jolliest* of them all is Robin.
(b) The *taller* of the twins is David.
(c) Either steel or brass can be used; steel is the *cheaper*.
(d) Bind it with string or wire, whichever is the *more convenient*.
(e) The *most dependable* girl in the class is Stella.

(f) He was the *friendliest* person I have ever met.
(g) Weigh them both and tell me which is the *heavier*.
(h) Either of these frocks would suit you, but the pink one is the *prettier*.
(i) His was the *most striking* picture in the exhibition.
(j) My left eye is the *weaker* one.
(k) He was the *most intrepid* climber in the party.
(l) You will find two basins on the shelf; bring me the *smaller*.

5. (a) Who did *most* work; Jim, Carl, or Michael?
(b) Which gives you *more* satisfaction, classical music or jazz?
(c) Alan works harder than David, but David has the *more* intelligence.
(d) Look through all the sheds in the catalogue, and order the one with the *most* floor-space.
(e) When you have thought about every occupation that may suit you, choose the one that will bring you the *most* happiness in life.
(f) Which country has *more* coast-line, Norway or Sweden?
(g) Mark Elizabeth's homework as well as Oliver's, and tell me who has the *more* mistakes.
(h) Consider both possibilities, and ask yourself which offers the *more* chance of success.

6. (a) Ask to see all the stoves they have in stock, and find out which one uses *least* fuel.
(b) Which motor cycle makes *less* noise, Ralph's or Leslie's?
(c) Which county has *less* rainfall, Lancashire or Norfolk?

25

(*d*) The children were fairly well-behaved, but Colin gave the *least* trouble of all.

(*e*) Which need *less* upkeep, steel window-frames or wooden ones?

(*f*) Of the two materials I prefer this one because it contains *less* cotton.

7. (*a*) The *sharper* the knife, the *cleaner* the cut.

(*b*) The *richer* the soil, the *heavier* the crop.

(*c*) The *brighter* the light, the *shorter* the exposure.

(*d*) The *nearer* the bone, the *sweeter* the meat.

(*e*) The *thinner* the china, the *more fragile* the cup.

(*f*) The *clearer* the air, the *more distant* the view.

(*g*) The *more violent* the storm, the *greater* the damage.

(*h*) The *more plentiful* the supply, the *lower* the price.

(*i*) The *more wicked* the crime, the *more severe* the punishment.

(*j*) The *more industrious* the nation, the *more prosperous* the people.

PAGE 38

8. (*a*) The *more hurried* the work, the *less accurate* the results.

(*b*) The *more numerous* the rooms, the *less convenient* the house.

(*c*) The *thicker* the legs, the *less graceful* the table.

(*d*) The *harder* the metal, the *less pliable* the wire.

(*e*) The *more interesting* the scenery, the *less tiring* the journey.

(*f*) The *greater* the altitude, the *less* the air pressure.

9.
endless	square	invisible
dead	daily	level
complete	silent	parallel
final	perpetual	immovable
identical	supreme	punctual
empty	true	infallible
ceaseless	innocent	

19. PREPOSITIONS

1. SUGGESTED ANSWERS

(*a*) I am surprised *at* you.

(*b*) You may rely *on* me to help you.

(*c*) The mongoose is not afraid *of* snakes.

(*d*) Lacrosse is similar *to* hockey.

(*e*) Who has been interfering *with* these tools?

(*f*) I know I can depend *upon* you.

(*g*) She was accompanied *by* her mother.

(*h*) I am accustomed *to* heat.

(*i*) I was encouraged *by* his praise.

(*j*) Please refrain *from* smoking.

(*k*) Are you satisfied *with* your new car?

(*l*) She cared *for* the wounded.

(*m*) May I confide *in* you?

(*n*) Never shrink *from* your duty.

(*o*) You must be thankful *for* your escape.

(*p*) He is not worthy *of* such a reward.

2. (*a*) She was unable to take part in the game because she was feeling *off* colour.

(*b*) Have you an ear *for* music?

(*c*) It goes *against* the grain for me to have to lend him money.

(*d*) Strike out on your own, and do not be content to go *with* the stream.

(*e*) He is a desperate character who would stick *at* nothing.

(*f*) Tell me the truth, without beating *about* the bush.

3. (Illustrated exercise)

SUGGESTED ANSWERS

(1) by	(9) off *or* into
(2) round	(10) after
(3) over	(11) across
(4) up	(12) against
(5) down	(13) among(st)
(6) through	(14) under
(7) to *or* towards	(15) between
(8) behind *or* in	(16) above

4. (*a*) His letter does not actually contain any complaints, but I can read *between* the lines.
   (*b*) The army attacked without warning, and took the city *by* storm.
   (*c*) You should have said that earlier; anyone can be wise *after* the event.
   (*d*) It is *on* the cards that we shall go to Italy.
   (*e*) Our village is *behind* the times; we still have no piped water.
   (*f*) Give him your opinion fearlessly, straight *from* the shoulder.
   (*g*) You can trust him; he is *above* board in all his dealings.
   (*h*) If you live *beyond* your means you will find yourself in difficulties sooner or later.
   (*i*) He finally reduced the price of the caravan by £10, and gave us the crockery *into* the bargain.
   (*j*) The farmer offered the Scouts the use of his barn to tide them *over* their difficulty.

(*k*) He admits his mistake, so there is no need to throw it *in* his teeth.
(*l*) You should think carefully, and not jump *to* conclusions.
(*m*) At the outbreak of war they had only a few thousand men *under* arms.
(*n*) Do not go too far away; I want you to stay *within* call.

5. (*a*) Bring a knife *with which* to sharpen your pencil.
   (*b*) I was given a locker *in which* to keep my books.
   (*c*) It is the manager *to whom* I wish to speak.
   (*d*) I could not see anything *behind which* to hide.
   (*e*) This is the chart *by which* they steered.
   (*f*) Tennis is the only game *at which* I am any good.
   (*g*) He is a man *for whom* I have the greatest respect.
   (*h*) She is a person *under whom* I should not like to work.
   F. D. & C. Manual, p. 49

6. (*a*) Which hotel are you staying *at*?
   (*b*) Which drawer have you put the thimble *in*?
   (*c*) Is this the book (that) you were telling me *about*?
   (*d*) Was it you (that) she was angry *with*?
   (*e*) Patrick is a boy (that) I thought I could depend *on*.
   (*f*) He lent me the hose-pipe (that) he washes the car *with*.
   (*g*) Flax is the plant that linen is made *from*.
   (*h*) I will give you the address of the

dealers (that) I had my stamps *from*.

(*i*) The police asked us if he was the man (that) we had been looking *for*.

(*j*) Tell me who it was (that) you spoke *to*.

(*k*) There is the ledge (that) we had to crawl *along*.

(*l*) Is this the road (that) we came in *by*?

See Note on p. 24.

PAGE 41

📖 LOOK THESE UP

I. (*a*) He stood *irresolute* at the water's edge.

(*b*) His writing is almost *illegible*.

(*c*) A landslide has made the road *impassable*.

(*d*) These ties are quite *inexpensive*.

2. Double negative

SUGGESTED ALTERNATIVES

I have brought nothing to eat.
I have not brought anything to eat.

3. When that hour came to him among the pines, he wakened thirsty. His tin was standing by him half full of water. He emptied it at a draught.

4. (*a*) transitively   (*d*) intransitively
(*b*) transitively   (*e*) transitively
(*c*) intransitively   (*f*) intransitively

5. (*a*) The stars were .... jewel-like.
(*b*) The cock first crows .... like a cheerful watchman.

6. (*a*) 1. .... changes in the face of Nature.

2. .... Nature breathing deeply and freely; even as she takes her rest, she turns and smiles.

3. .... the sleeping hemisphere.

(*b*) The .... talk of the runnel.

7. who
houseless men

8. stirring, sleeping

9. (i) on the meadows
(ii) on dewy hill-sides
(iii) to a new lair among the ferns

PAGE 42

20. AGREEMENT

I. (*a*) *Is/Was* there a box for these dominoes?

(*b*) *Has* there been a reduction in prices?

(*c*) *Are/Were* there any gloves on the window-ledge?

(*d*) *Were* there telephones a hundred years ago?

(*e*) *Is/Was* there anyone upstairs?

(*f*) *Are* there a hundred pence in a pound?

(*g*) *Are/Were* there any books in the cupboard?

(*h*) *Have* there been any wood-pigeons in the garden?

2. (*a*) *There are* a thousand pictures in this art gallery.

(*b*) *There was* a monastery here five hundred years ago.

(*c*) *There were* sunflowers and holly-hocks in her garden.

(*d*) *There is* gold in these mountains.

28

(e) *There are* concerts here several times a week.

(f) *There were* six men in the expedition.

(g) *There was* a clump of trees on the hill-top.

(h) *There was* a crowd of people in the market-place.

3. (a) Each of us *was* questioned.

(b) Each of my brothers *is* taking a turn.

(c) Every one of you must behave like *a man*.

(d) Every one of these chisels *looks* blunt.

(e) Each of the hats *bears a label* saying that *it has* been reduced to half price.

(f) Each of the animals *has* been shut up in *its* own *pen*.

(g) Every one of these envelopes *has* dirty marks on *it*.

(h) Every one of the boys *was* expected to make *his* own *bed*.

F. D. & C. Manual, p. 37

4. (a) Either of these lamp-shades *is* suitable.

(b) Neither of these scarves *is* mine.

(c) Neither of my parents *has* yet seen my report.

(d) *Was* either of the applicants suitable?

(e) Neither of these *is* worth considering.

(f) I hope that neither of these ropes *breaks*.

(g) *Has* either of these stair carpets any red in *it*?

(h) Neither of the grocers in our village *has* electric light in *his shop*.

(i) Call me when either of the bells *rings*.

(j) *Does* either of the girls make *her* own dresses?

F. D. & C. Manual, p. 37

5. (a) One of his eyes *was* injured.

(b) The cupboard under the stairs *is* dark.

(c) The eggs lying in the dry sand *are* almost invisible.

(d) A photograph of the prizewinners *has* been taken.

(e) A copy of the rules *was* pinned up.

(f) Many songs from this opera *are* still popular.

(g) This book of operatic songs *is* still popular.

(h) The tallest of the three boys *is* John.

(i) Pipes from the strainer *carry* away the syrup.

(j) The movement of her arms *was* most graceful.

6. (a) Among the trees *stands* a statue.

(b) On the promenade *are* two kiosks.

(c) Behind the curtains *hangs* a cord.

(d) On this bush *grow* pale yellow flowers.

(e) In that mountain range *rise* two well-known rivers.

(f) Which socks *is* Colin to have?

(g) At the end of three weeks *comes* a holiday of two days.

(h) What emotions *does* a man feel when faced by death?

7. (a) All the animals, with the exception of one pony, *were* brought out before the roof collapsed.

(b) The festival, contrary to expectations, *has* made a profit.

(c) This road, divided into six lanes, *carries* most of the north-bound traffic.

(d) An outbreak of fowl pest, involving five hundred birds, *has* been reported.

(e) The new president, like his brothers, *is* well known for *his* skill at polo.

(f) The uninjured passengers, including Sir John Craig, *were* able to continue *their* journey.

(g) Drier weather, with some showers, *is* expected to spread to all areas.

(h) The choir, of two hundred voices, *was* formed five years ago.

F. D. & C. Manual, p. 27 (apposition)

8. (a) Put it in the oven for baby and *me*.

(b) Can Elizabeth and *I* sit here?

(c) You and *I* are the only ones without raincoats.

(d) The coach drove off and left Gwen and *me* behind.

(e) Carl and Joan are playing against Robert and *me*.

(f) Kathleen and *I* decorated the room; the cakes were made by Mildred and *me*.

(g) Brian, Alan, Gerald, and *I* were all born in June.

(h) This snowman was made by Eric and *me*; Frank and *I* are going to make another one.

(i) In front of my father and *me* sat the president and his wife.

(j) It was to Howard and *me* that these rabbits were given.

F. D. & C. Manual, p. 41

PAGE 44

9. (a) Either dogs *or* foxes could have done this.

(b) Neither the hat *nor* the coat belongs to me.

(c) He can neither bat *nor* bowl.

(d) You may do the picture either in water-colour *or* in pencil.

(e) She neither saw *nor* heard anyone.

(f) This might be either silk *or* rayon; it is definitely neither cotton *nor* linen.

(g) Her holiday is either in May *or* in June.

(h) I shall neither buy him a new satchel *nor* pay for the repair of the old one.

(i) This cannot possibly be either mahogany *or* teak.

(j) I shall not lend him either my bat *or* my pads.

F. D. & C. Manual, p. 37

★ REVISION

I. (a) The *quickest* of three ways

(b) The *slower* of two trains

(c) The *most foolish* of ten people

(d) The *most courteous* of five boys

(e) The *more experienced* of two leaders

(f) The *more memorable* of two occasions

2. (a) You must not go swimming either in the pool *or* in the river.

(b) Each of the bedrooms *has its* own separate bathroom.

(c) Tom, with his sisters, *is* coming later.

21. RELATIVE PRONOUNS

1. (a) Here is a child *whose* knee is bleeding.
   (b) Morphia, *which* is a dangerous drug, cannot be obtained without a prescription.
   (c) Is there anyone from *whom* I can borrow a pencil?
   (d) I do not know *what* they have decided to do.
   (e) Ask the teacher *who* takes you for English.
   (f) Make a list of all the things *that**
   you have bought.

* Fowler, in *Modern English Usage*, has an interesting article on the use of *that* and *which* in this context.

2. (a) The French were led by Joan of Arc, *who* was only a young girl.
   (b) This picture shows the Sandwich Islands, *which* were discovered by Captain Cook.
   (c) St. Paul's Cathedral was built by Wren, *whose* tomb can be seen in the crypt.
   (d) The Roman invaders were defeated by Boadicea, *who* was queen of the Iceni tribe.
   (e) Columbus encountered the Sargasso Sea, *which* is a mass of floating seaweed.
   (f) Another early aviator was Blériot, *who* was the first to fly across the English Channel.
   (g) George VI was followed by Elizabeth II, *whose* coronation took place in 1953.
   (h) Napoleon was defeated at Waterloo, *which* is near Brussels.

   (i) The finest tenor at that time was Caruso, *whose* fame was world-wide.

   F. D. & C. Manual, p. 51

PAGE 45

3. (a) The purple grapes, *which* hung just out of his reach, were a great temptation to the fox.
   (b) The hare, *who* had been asleep all day, was amazed to find that the tortoise had reached the winning-post before him.
   (c) When the peasant picked up the egg, *which* shone in the morning sunlight, he saw that it was made of pure gold.
   (d) The mouse, *whose* life had once been spared by the lion, was able to free the lion by gnawing through the ropes that held him.
   (e) The jar, *which* had a long neck, was too deep for the fox to reach any of the frog stew.
   (f) The young mouse, *whose* suggestion had been received with delight, had not thought of how the bell was to be tied round the cat's neck.
   (g) The shepherds, *who* had already been hoaxed twice by the foolish boy, took no notice when they again heard the cry of 'Wolf!'

4. (a) Dennis   (e) lid
   (b) Eric   (f) tennis
   (c) Chester   (g) boy
   (d) cat   (h) girl

5. SUGGESTED ANSWERS
   (a) *The cage is said to be able to talk.*
       In a cage I have a parrot that can talk.

31

(b) *The boy is said to have a beard.*

We saw an old man, whose beard was white and bushy, with a little boy.

(c) *The birthday is said to wind itself.*

For my birthday, father bought me a watch that winds itself automatically.

(d) *The parents are said to be under five years of age.*

Children under five years of age, in charge of parents, are admitted free.

(e) *The bread is said to have been made a hundred years ago.*

We have a cupboard, made a hundred years ago, for storing bread.

(f) *It is said that the house should be sent to the surveyor.*

Fill in the form, giving the required information about your house, and send it to the surveyor.

(g) *The dogs, not their owners, seem to be expressing the wish.*

Visitors who wish to come into the park with dogs must keep them under control.

(h) *The people are said to have bowed to the horse.*

The queen, to whom all the people bowed low, rode out on a fine black horse.

6. SUGGESTED ANSWERS

(a) The gorilla, which climbs trees in search of food, lives in the African forest.

(b) Queen Mary, who was one of the daughters of Henry VIII, married Philip of Spain.

(c) Jason, whose companions were known as the Argonauts, set out in search of the Golden Fleece.

(d) Marconi showed the king the instrument with which he had sent messages across the Atlantic.

(e) Any bee that strays in from another colony is killed or driven out of the hive.

(f) Norfolk, to which thousands of visitors go each year, still has many quiet and unfrequented villages.

7. (a) 1. Bob Cratchit tried to warm himself at the candle, *which* was brighter than the fire.
2. Bob Cratchit, *who* shivered in his dismal little cell, tried to warm himself at the candle.

(b) 1. Bob wore a long comforter, *which* hung down before him.
2. Bob, *whose* threadbare clothes were darned and brushed, wore a long comforter.

(c) 1. The pudding, *which* was like a speckled cannon-ball, was carried in proudly by Mrs. Cratchit.
2. The pudding was carried in proudly by Mrs. Cratchit, *whose* face was flushed and smiling.

(d) 1. The smaller Cratchits had smelt the goose, *which* was being cooked at the baker's.
2. The smaller Cratchits, *who* had stood outside the baker's shop, had smelt the goose.

(e) 1. The active little crutch, *which* was heard at that moment upon the floor, was that of Tiny Tim.

2. The active little crutch was that of Tiny Tim, *whose* limbs were supported by an iron frame.

NOTE. A further useful exercise is the combination of all three elements into a single sentence, thus:—*Bob Cratchit, who shivered in his dismal little cell, tried to warm himself at the candle, which was brighter than the fire.*

8. (*a*) They saw a blackbird's nest, *in which* were four eggs.
   (*b*) At the end of the room was a fire-place, *above which* hung a large mirror.
   (*c*) At the top of the cylinder is a valve, *through which* oxygen is introduced.
   (*d*) Firing-practice is indicated by a red flag, *beyond which* we are not allowed to go.
   (*e*) Outside stood a new fire-engine, *round which* a crowd had already gathered.
   (*f*) From beneath his cloak he drew a flute, *on which* he began to play a slow sad tune.

9. (*a*) His favourite pastime was archery, *at which* he was highly skilled.
   (*b*) The garden was alive with cater-pillars, *of which* there seemed to be millions.
   (*c*) At the back of the car is a coupling, *to which* a caravan can be attached.
   (*d*) They are now drilling through a layer of shale, *beneath which* they expect to find petroleum.
   (*e*) The water swirled me against a slimy post, *around which* I flung my arms desperately.
   (*f*) The entrance to the cave was a narrow slit, *through which* we wriggled with difficulty.

PAGE 47

10.(*a*) Concealed behind the curtain he found a small cupboard, *inside which hung* a rusty key.
   (*b*) In the middle of the hall was a round table, *round which sat* the king and his knights.
   (*c*) His attention was attracted by an oak chest, *against which leaned* a cross-bow.
   (*d*) At the west end is a statue of Bishop Gray *beside which stands* an ancient font.
   (*e*) A few palm-trees mark the edge of the oasis, *beyond which lies* empty and barren desert.
   (*f*) Between the mountains is a broad plain, *across which meanders* a sluggish river.

11.(*a*) A bottle, *inside which a letter could be seen*, was found at the water's edge.
   (*b*) The tunnel, *through which hundreds of cars pass daily*, is five kilometres long.
   (*c*) The wall, *across which is a wide crack*, is in danger of falling.
   (*d*) This hotel, *beyond which there is nothing but sand and sea*, is said to be the last hotel in Spain.
   (*e*) Castle Hill, *from which can be seen nine counties*, is the highest point in the district.
   (*f*) The town, *near which there were abundant supplies of coal and clay*, became famous for its pottery.

12.(*a*) Stella is a good-natured girl *for whom* I have a great admiration.

(b) Mr. Quinn was an old man <u>from whom</u> the children bought puppets.

(c) Andrew Dahl was a botanist <u>after whom</u> the dahlia was named.

(d) Monsieur and Madame Curie were scientists <u>of whom</u> few people had ever heard.

(e) Huddled against the wall was a woman <u>beside whom</u> a small child lay.

(f) Did you notice the very tall lady <u>behind whom</u> I was sitting?

(g) Gerald is an easy-going boy <u>to whom</u> nothing comes as a surprise.

(h) Handel was a composer <u>by whom</u> some of the world's greatest music was written.

(i) Captain Jones was the commander <u>under whom</u> my brother served.

(j) Socrates was a great philosopher <u>with whom</u> many people studied.

13.(a) The king gave the golden bell to his youngest daughter, *whom* he loved dearly.

(b) The governor of Egypt was Joseph, *whom* none of the brothers recognized.

(c) All eyes turned upon Gustav, *whom* Rupert had thrust to the doorway.

(d) At a table in the corner sat a young man *whom* the rest of the travellers avoided.

(e) Alarm was spreading among the villagers, *whom* Julian had told of the rebellion.

(f) The two rogues turned with whips upon the helpless merchant, *whom* they had tied to the wheel of his own cart.

(g) So they took sticks and went in search of Kriska, *whom* everyone called a witch.

(h) Rob handed the letter to Dick, *whom* Rob regarded as a trustworthy messenger.

14.(a) Two bystanders, *whom the police are anxious to trace*, are known to have witnessed the accident.

(b) Mrs. Parker, *whom no-one has yet beaten*, is thus within sight of winning two championships.

(c) A young woman, *whom the rescue party was unable to identify*, was found lying on the ledge.

(d) Mr. Faulkner, *whom the bandits are holding to ransom*, is a retired civil servant.

(e) The Chancellor, *whom the Prime Minister saw last night*, will make a statement in the Commons today.

(f) Mr. Scott, *whom the society has chosen as its first president*, is an architect by profession.

(g) Several young actors, *whom the producers have recently discovered*, will make their début in this play.

(h) Two doctors, *whom passers-by had told of the explosion*, immediately offered their services.

15.(a) These bees belong to the lady *who* lives next door.

(b) The man *whom* we suspected has been arrested.

(c) These are the people *whom* we admire.

(d) The architect *who* designed this church died yesterday.

(e) She is the only person *whom* I can recommend.

(f) The children *whom* she had taught were there to say good-bye.

34

(g) I am unable to say *who* the culprit is.

(h) Is he the juggler *whom* we saw on television?

16.(a) Choose four boys *who* you know are reliable.

(b) Choose four boys *whom* you know to be reliable.

(c) The progress prize goes to Yvonne, *whom* I believe to be the most deserving girl in the class.

(d) The progress prize goes to Yvonne, *who* I feel sure has earned it.

(e) Give the job to a man *whom* you can trust to do it well.

(f) Give the job to a man *who* you are sure will do it well.

(g) The captain will be Alec, *who* we consider is well worthy of the position.

(h) The captain will be Alec, *whom* we consider well worthy of the position.

F. D. & C. Manual, p. 57

See Note on p. 24 of this book.

22. VOICE

I. (a) The ball was handled by Payton.

(b) The drowning boy was rescued by a passer-by.

(c) The weather is studied by meteorologists.

(d) More money will be spent by the customers.

(e) An apology will be written by Molly.

(f) Serious accidents can be caused by landslides.

2. (a) In 1884 the turbine was invented by Parsons.

(b) Tomorrow morning the memorial will be unveiled by the Prime Minister.

(c) Because he had no licence, the driver was prosecuted by the police.

(d) At the end of the lecture the professor was cheered by the audience.

(e) At night I am tormented by mosquitoes.

(f) Until he is eighteen he will be maintained by his parents.

3. (a) Clive's uncle caught these trout.

(b) Rioters damaged several buildings.

(c) Rockets can reach outer space.

(d) Mr. Parsons will take the wedding photographs.

(e) The treasurer should bank the money immediately.

(f) Natives sometimes bring gifts.

F. D. & C. Manual, p. 56

4. (a) These particulars must be printed in block capitals.

(b) This lift must not be used without written authority.

(c) This form should be completed and returned to the office.

(d) Dogs may not be brought into the store.

(e) Tickets must be shown to the inspector on request.

(f) Umbrellas should be left in the cloak-room.

5. (a) The price of coal should be reduced.

(b) The fire station should be improved.

(c) We were told that we should have a new school.
(d) We were promised lower taxation.
(e) We were given no say in the matter.
(f) When will swimming-baths be built for the children?

LOOK THESE UP

1. Diminutives
-ling, -ette, -et, -ule.

2. crazier; most precious

3. (a) My father thinks nothing of walking fifty kilometres.
(b) Send your reply on a postcard to reach us not later than Monday.
(c) I spent the whole of yesterday weeding the garden.

23. PHRASES AND CLAUSES

1. (a) Phrase   (f) Clause
   (b) Phrase   (g) Clause
   (c) Clause   (h) Phrase
   (d) Clause   (i) Phrase
   (e) Phrase   (j) Clause

2. (a) why you are angry
   (b) that the train was late
   (c) that he was a cowboy
   (d) what you told me
   (e) how I can loosen this screw

PAGE 51

3. (a) What he saw
   (b) How the accident happened
   (c) Whatever I suggest
   (d) Why he blushed
   (e) That he will recover completely

4. (a) that I could swim (object)
   (b) What she did (subject)
   (c) what I had been asked to do (object)
   (d) how he could mend his air-gun (object)
   (e) How the lion escaped (subject)
   (f) Why he said such a stupid thing (subject)

F. D. & C. Manual, p. 46

5. SUGGESTED ANSWERS

   (a) A boy *without shoes* was standing outside the door.
   (b) I prefer a coat *with a belt*.
   (c) The guardsman, *unbelievably tall*, stooped at the low doorway.
   (d) The coupons, *given free in every packet*, can be exchanged for valuable presents.
   (e) In the top drawer you will find a tool *for opening bottles*.
   (f) This wine is made from grapes *grown in Germany*.

F. D. & C. Manual, p. 24

6. SUGGESTED ANSWERS

   (a) **mistletoe.** An evergreen plant <u>that grows on apple trees</u>.
   (b) **porcupine.** A gnawing animal <u>with a prickly back</u>.
   (c) **tartan.** Woollen cloth <u>with a coloured check pattern</u>.
   (d) **planet.** A heavenly body <u>that moves around the sun</u>.
   (e) **orange.** A juicy fruit <u>with a reddish-yellow skin</u>.
   (f) **privet.** An evergreen shrub <u>used for hedges</u>.
   (g) **mildew.** A fluffy growth <u>that appears on damp things</u>.

(h) **mammoth.** A huge elephant, now extinct.

7. SUGGESTED ANSWERS

(a) He can climb a rope *like a monkey.*
(b) *After lunch* we are going to the circus.
(c) We were awake *before sunrise.*
(d) Meet me *at the cross-roads.*
(e) No spectators are allowed *during rehearsal.*
(f) I punished Rover *for clawing the arm-chair.*

F. D. & C. Manual, p. 25

PAGE 52

8. (a) Compound   (f) Complex
   (b) Complex   (g) Compound
   (c) Complex   (h) Compound
   (d) Compound   (i) Simple
   (e) Simple   (j) Complex

24. PARTICIPLES

1. (a) whistling (*adj.*) (e) swimming (*v.*)
   (b) darning (*v.*)   (f) galloping (*adj.*)
   (c) dripping (*adj.*)   (g) flying (*v.*)
   (d) dancing (*adj.*)   (h) walking (*v.*)

2. (a) *Collecting* their belongings, they went back home.
   (b) *Looking* northwards we saw strange lights in the sky.
   (c) *Holding* the child shoulder-high he waded into the flood.
   (d) *Saying* that he would be away for some time, he stumbled out of the tent.
   (e) *Thinking* he had won, he stopped running.

(f) *Seeing* that there was no hope of escape, I gave myself up.

3. (a) "This is our shop, Nickleby," said Squeers, *stepping* into the school.
   (b) Mrs. Squeers stood at one of the desks, *presiding* over an immense basin of brimstone and treacle.
   (c) "I was driven to do it," said Smike faintly, *casting* another imploring look about him.
   (d) "Stop!" cried Nicholas, *starting* up and *stepping* forward.
   (e) Squeers fell violently, *striking* his head against a form in his descent.

PAGE 53

4. (a) *Rushing* into the room in great excitement, *Mr. Bumble* cried, "Oliver Twist has asked for more!"
   (b) *Deciding* that he would stand it no longer, *Oliver* slipped out of the shop and ran away.
   (c) *Giving* Oliver a shilling, *Fagin* said, "You're a clever boy, my dear."
   (d) *Plunging* his hand into the gentleman's pocket, *the Dodger* drew out a handkerchief.
   (e) *Pointing* to the door with his pistol, *Sikes* told Oliver that if he faltered he would shoot him.

F. D. & C. Manual, p. 47

5. (a) stolen (*v.*)   (e) batted (*v.*)
   (b) drawn (*v.*)   (f) known (*adj.*)
   (c) knitted (*adj.*)   (g) bent (*adj.*)
   (d) driven (*adj.*)   (h) laid (*v.*)

6. (a) have begun   (f) had forgotten
   (b) are chosen   (g) were stolen
   (c) was swum   (h) is broken
   (d) am known   (i) having wakened
   (e) has rung

37

7. (a) *Shaken* by the earthquake, chimneys tottered and fell.
   (b) *Forsaken* by the tribe, the old man trudged on alone.
   (c) *Trodden* into the soft turf, the brooch had passed unnoticed for weeks.
   (d) *Sunk* in a collision with an iceberg, the Titanic carried nearly 1500 people to their deaths.
   (e) *Shrunk* by a special process, these shirts will retain their shape.
   (f) *Taken* from the factory yard on Saturday, the lorry was found on Monday in Norwich.
   (g) *Sung* by generations of children, these tunes are as popular today as ever they were.

PAGE 54

8. SUGGESTED ANSWERS

   (a) *It was not the puzzle that followed the instructions.*
   Following the instructions, I found the puzzle easy.
   (b) *It was not the road that was hobbling.*
   The road seemed endless as I hobbled on blistered feet.
   (c) *It was not the duel that was bleeding.*
   When the contestants were bleeding from wounds in their arms, the the duel was brought to an end.
   (d) *It was not the view that was climbing.*
   The view became more extensive as we climbed up the hillside.
   (e) *It was not the journey that was wrapped in warm clothes.*
   Wrapped in warm clothes, I thoroughly enjoyed the journey.
   (f) *It was not the task that was discouraged.*
   Discouraged by many difficulties,

I thought the task was hopeless.
   (g) *It was not the competition that hoped for a prize.*
   Hoping for a big prize, I get a thrill from the competition.
   (h) *It is not the matter that is making the request.*
   Requesting you to pay this account immediately, we must inform you that the matter will be put in the hands of our solicitor if there is further delay.

9. (a) Was there any danger of *his* being killed?
   (b) The water leaked away without *our* noticing it.
   (c) Did they give any reason for *their* leaving?
   (d) Do you mind *my* smoking?
   (e) I am thankful for *your* helping me.
   (f) I cannot understand *their* forgetting us.

10.(a) Father caught *me* climbing the apple tree.
   (b) There is no hope of *our* being chosen.
   (c) I saw *him* being helped to his feet.
   (d) The picture fell without *my* touching it.
   (e) I cannot agree to *your* breaking the rules.
   (f) They watched *us* launching the boat.

📖 **LOOK THESE UP**

1. (a) Pun. (b) Euphemism.
   (c) Ambiguity.

2. membership, kindness, manhood, criticism, shortness or shortage, justice or justness, vandalism, partnership.

38

25. THE PARTS OF SPEECH

I. SUGGESTED ANSWERS

(a) To set up or establish (*verb*)
(b) A distance of about three miles (*noun*)
(c) One and only (*adjective*)
(d) To thump or crush (*verb*)
(e) A strait (*noun*)
(f) A short period (*noun*)
(g) A noisy quarrel or fight (*noun*)
(h) To be faithful (*verb*)
(i) Left-hand (*adjective*)
(j) To sink deliberately (*verb*)

2.

ADJECTIVE Mr. X is ...	ADVERB He behaves ...	NOUN He is noted for his ...
bold	boldly	boldness
honest	honestly	honesty
modest	modestly	modesty
mean	meanly	meanness
violent	violently	violence
wicked	wickedly	wickedness
brave	bravely	bravery
stupid	stupidly	stupidity
angry	angrily	anger
plucky	pluckily	pluck
efficient	efficiently	efficiency
wise	wisely	wisdom
prudent	prudently	prudence
humble	humbly	humility or humbleness

3.
1. noun	4. adverb	7. noun
2. adverb	5. adjective	8. adverb
3. noun	6. adjective	9. adjective

4.

VERB	ADJECTIVE	ADVERB	NOUN
economize	economical	economically	economy
agree	agreeable	agreeably	agreement
boast	boastful	boastfully	boastfulness
differ	different	differently	difference
amaze	amazing	amazingly	amazement
excite*	exciting	excitingly	excitement
play	playful	playfully	playfulness
pity	pitiful	pitifully	pity
irritate	irritable	irritably	irritability
rely	reliable	reliably	reliability
prefer	preferable	preferably	preference
enjoy	enjoyable	enjoyably	enjoyment
satisfy	satisfactory	satisfactorily	satisfaction
admire	admirable	admirably	admiration
hurry	hurried	hurriedly	hurry
obey	obedient	obediently	obedience
deceive	deceitful	deceitfully	deceit
doubt	doubtful	doubtfully	doubtfulness
defy	defiant	defiantly	defiance

* NOTE: Alternative answers may be expected in some instances; e.g., the pupil may hesitate between *exciting* and *excitable*. With a few exceptions the given word supplies the key; that is to say, *irritable* should lead to *irritability* rather than to *irritation*.

5. SUGGESTED ANSWERS

(a) 1. magnificent = splendid (*adjective*)

2. magnificence = splendour (*noun*)
3. magnificently = splendidly (*adverb*)

(*b*) 1. stubbornly = doggedly (*adverb*)
2. stubbornness = doggedness (*noun*)
3. stubborn = dogged (*adjective*)

(*c*) 1. exactness = accuracy (*noun*)
2. exactly = accurately (*adverb*)
3. exact = accurate (*adjective*)

(*d*) 1. indolence = laziness (*noun*)
2. indolent = lazy (*adjective*)
3. indolently = lazily (*adverb*)

(*e*) 1. awkwardness = clumsiness (*noun*)
2. awkwardly = clumsily (*adverb*)
3. awkward = clumsy (*adjective*)

(*f*) 1. feeble = weak (*adjective*)
2. feebleness = weakness (*noun*)
3. feebly = weakly (*adverb*)

(*g*) 1. foolishly = senselessly (*adverb*)
2. foolishness = senselessness (*noun*)
3. foolish = senseless (*adjective*)

(*h*) 1. careful = cautious (*adjective*)
2. carefully = cautiously (*adverb*)
3. care = caution (*noun*)

(*i*) 1. danger = peril (*noun*)
2. dangerous = perilous (*adjective*)
3. dangerously = perilously (*adverb*)

PAGE 57

6. 1. cottage, breakfast
2. took, went, fell
3. axes or trees
4. Edward, Humphrey
5. young
6. helped, put, returned
7. new
8. cluster
9. gun, path
10. and
11. He, we
12. which
13. small
14. Ah!
15. had, should
16. eagerness
17. they
18. days, inclosure
19. have, took, came, knew
20. which
21. in, to
22. cheerfully
23. and
24. I
25. help, consented
26. on
27. venison, cart
28. was
29. that
30. gladly
31. would, have
32. so
33. him
34. some
35. with, to
36. out
37. few
38. then
39. off
40. at
41. you, I
42. feeding-ground
43. spruce-fir
44. now, down
45. running
46. marked
47. Noun
48. Verb
49. Noun
50. Adjective
51. Noun
52. Verb
53. Noun
54. Noun
55. Noun
56. Preposition
57. Adverb
58. Pronoun
59. Preposition
60. Adverb

PAGE 58

7. 1. noun
2. adjective
3. verb (transitive)
4. adjective
5. adjective
6. verb (transitive)
7. noun
8. adjective
9. adjective
10. noun; imagination
11. noun; ticket of admission
12. verb (transitive)
13. verb (transitive)
14. noun; sea
15. interjection
16. verb (transitive)
17. adjective
18. preposition
19. adjective
20. verb (transitive)
21. interjection
22. adjective; harsh
23. noun; perfume
24. adjective; right and honest

40

25. noun; swoon
26. verb (transitive)
27. noun
28. adjective
29. noun; stillness (or quietness)
30. adjective; horizontal
31. verb (intransitive)
32. noun; glad reception
33. adjective
34. noun; stage in a competition
35. verb (intransitive); run with water
36. verb (transitive)
37. preposition
38. noun
39. noun
40. noun
41. adjective
42. noun
43. noun; sensitive flesh
44. noun
45. noun; small portion
46. verb (intransitive)
47. verb (transitive); slacken
48. verb (transitive); approaching
49. verb (intransitive); wedged
50. adjective; friendly
51. adverb
52. noun; judgement of style
53. adjective
54. verb (intransitive)
55. verb (transitive)
56. verb (transitive)
57. adverb; still (even now)
58. noun
59. adverb; strenuously
60. pronoun
61. interjection
62. conjunction
63. noun
64. pronoun
65. verb (intransitive); change position.
66. adjective
67. verb (intransitive)
68. verb (intransitive)
69. adverb
70. verb (intransitive)
71. conjunction; during the time that
72. adverb; firmly
73. adverb; correctly
74. noun; space of time
75. adverb
76. verb (transitive)

★ REVISION

1. Mr. John Holt thanks Miss K. Shaw for inviting *him* to *her* birthday party, but regrets that owing to the serious illness of *his* parents *he* will be unable to be present.

2. (a) These particulars must be written in ink.
   (b) Cars may not be parked here.
   (c) This column should be left blank.

3. (a) Each of them *was* interviewed.
   (b) Beneath these waters *lies* a galleon.
   (c) Neither Tom nor Pat *is* related to me.
   (d) Either of these needles *is* suitable.
   (e) Joy, as well as Sally, *is* coming.

4. SUGGESTED ANSWERS
   (a) Brighton was crowded with visitors enjoying the fine weather.
   (b) At ten thousand metres the sky was blue and cloudless.

5. (a) Pick someone *whom* you know to be honest.
   (b) This year we have a team of athletes *who* we hope will break many records.

6. (a) steadily, lightly
   (b) fir-points or pack-saddle (noun)
      jewel-like (adjective)
      stock-still (adverb)
   (c) (i) by   (ii) under   (iii) between
   (d) world are
   (e) The pronoun *it* stands instead of the noun *night*.

41

SECTION TWO
PUNCTUATION

PAGE 61

26. BEGINNING AND ENDING A SENTENCE

1. Gorillas live in the tropical forests. They climb trees in search of food. When they are angry they beat their breasts. A single blow from a gorilla's paw can kill a man.

2. The jackdaw is very like the rook. It is sometimes kept as a pet. With patience it can be taught to speak. Jackdaws are mischievous birds. They carry off and hide any small glittering object.

3. I was born in a land of ice and snow. I had six brothers and two sisters. My father worked in the forest. I do not remember my mother. We were very poor. The winters were always bitterly cold. Sometimes we had nothing to eat. Then the little ones cried. We crouched together for warmth. Outside the wolves were howling. It was a hard and sad childhood.

27. CAPITAL LETTERS FOR PROPER NOUNS

1. (a) The largest county in England is Yorkshire.

(b) Yesterday we met Joyce Webb's uncle in Brighton.

(c) Last Tuesday I went to Windsor.

(d) My friend Alec lives in Mill Street.

(e) I spent Easter in Exeter with my brother John and his wife.

(f) The Pope sent a message to Roman Catholics throughout the world.

(g) If Wolverhampton Wanderers beat Manchester United they will meet West Bromwich Albion at Wembley.

(h) The biggest school in the town is Queen Mary's School.

PAGE 62

2. (a) Greater London Council
(b) Church of England
(c) Lord Mayor of London
(d) Edward the Confessor
(e) United States of America
(f) Victoria Cross
(g) Victoria and Albert Museum
(h) Justice of the Peace
(i) Her Royal Highness the Duchess of Kent
(j) The Royal Society for the Prevention of Cruelty to Animals

3. (a) Alice's Adventures in Wonderland
(b) The Adventures of Don Quixote

42

(c) Under the Greenwood Tree
(d) A Tale of Two Cities
(e) The Cloister and the Hearth
(f) Three Men in a Boat
(g) Round the World in Eighty Days

4. Mr. Thirlby's home is now in America, and he has brought his family over to see Britain. After a week in London they went to Oxford to visit Mr. Thirlby's old college (Christ Church); they then made for Stratford-on-Avon, where Adrian Healey and Frances Harman are appearing in "Romeo and Juliet". From Stratford they moved on to North Wales (Mr. Thirlby has a brother at Caernarvon), and they spent a few days in Snowdonia. Since Thursday they have been in the Lake District, and I understand that during the last week of August they intend to visit the Edinburgh Festival.

28. CAPITAL LETTERS IN POETRY

1. It was the time when lilies blow,
And clouds are highest up in air,
Lord Ronald brought a lily-white doe
To give his cousin, Lady Clare.

2. It was upon an April morn,
While yet the frost lay hoar,
We heard Lord James's bugle-horn
Sound by the rocky shore.

3. To you in David's town this day
Is born of David's line
A saviour, who is Christ the Lord;
And this shall be the sign.

29. ABBREVIATIONS
F. D. & C. Manual, p. 23

1. Automobile Association
Please turn over
Royal Navy
Fire hydrant
Royal Automobile Club
  or Royal Armoured Corps
Bachelor of Arts
Criminal Investigation Department
Greenwich Mean Time
Queen's Counsel
Young Men's Christian Association

2.

Ranks	Medals	Sport
Gen.	G.M.	F.A.
N.C.O.	G.C.	M.C.C.
Col.	V.C.	c. and b.
Lieut.	D.S.C.	l.b.w.
Maj.	M.C.	K.O.

Councils	Countries, etc.
G.L.C.	N.Z.
C.C.	U.K.
	N.S.W.

PAGE 63

3.

H.Q.	B.Sc.
Anon.	Hon. Sec.
Cdr.	cm.
per cent.	MS.
M.D.	M.

4.

Som.	Cambs.
Northants.	Beds.
Oxon.	Hants.
Salop	Wilts.
Berks.	Herts.

5. Thomas, Charles, George, William,

43

Henry, Frederick, James, Joseph or Josiah, John.

6. A.A.A.   V.I.P.   F.R.I.B.A.
   B.S.T.   M.F.H.   M.R.C.V.S.
   B.V.M.   N.A.A.F.I.   N.S.P.C.C.

7. The Rev. B. Matthews = D
   Edward Hollis, D.F.C. = I
   W. A. Dennis (Hon. Treas.) = B
   Nigel Watson, M.D. = C
   Bradbury of the C.I.D. = H
   Mlle Temple = E
   James Ross Snr. = G
   Maj. D. C. Rogers = A
   L. Thornton, M.A. (Cantab.) = J
   Sir Charles Roberts, Q.C. = F

8. **A.D.**   In the year of our Lord
   a.m.   Before noon
   i.e.   That is
   Messrs.   Gentlemen
   p.m.   After noon
   e.g.   For example
   N.B.   Note well
   v.   Against
   R.S.V.P.   Please reply

9. (a) Corinthians   (g) Matthew
   (b) Ephesians   (h) Philippians
   (c) Exodus   (i) Proverbs
   (d) Galatians   (j) Psalms
   (e) Genesis   (k) Revelation
   (f) Isaiah   (l) Romans

30. QUESTION-MARKS

1. (a) Vehicles must stop at a *Stop* sign.
   (b) Ostriches can run quickly.
   (c) Victoria was a famous queen.
   (d) The Vikings were great sailors.
   (e) Many expeditions have been to the Antarctic.

2. (a) Is the middle of the earth still molten?
   (b) Can a chameleon change colour?
   (c) Was the mammoth a long-tusked elephant?
   (d) Were these coral reefs made by tiny animals?
   (e) Are fossils of shell-fish found in rock?
   (f) Do the worker bees kill the drones at the end of the summer?
   (g) Did great tree-ferns grow in the swamps?

3. (a) Yes   (e) Yes
   (b) No   (f) No
   (c) No   (g) No
   (d) Yes   (h) Yes

4. (a) When do we break up?
   (b) I wonder how that trick is done.
   (c) Where is the salt?
   (d) Can Olive swim?
   (e) Tell me if this is wrong.
   (f) I want to know whose catapult this is.
   (g) Would you mind making less noise?
   (h) Say why you asked .that question.
   F. D. & C. Manual, p. 50

5. (a) Direct   (e) Indirect
   (b) Indirect   (f) Direct
   (c) Indirect   (g) Indirect
   (d) Direct   (h) Indirect

31. COMMAS

1. (a) The elm is one of our tallest trees. It has a thick and rugged trunk.

44

(b) Poplars grow very quickly. Their wood is neither strong nor durable.

(c) You can easily recognize the beech, for its bark is like smooth olive-grey metal.

(d) Because walnut takes a fine polish and does not split, high-class furniture is made from it.

(e) Oak trees are slow in growth. They live to a very great age.

(f) The yew was once a very important tree, its wood being used for making long-bows.

(g) Not easily harmed by smoke and fumes, the plane tree thrives in large cities.

2. [NOTE: Opinions differ concerning the insertion of a comma after the penultimate item in a series.]

(a) In my garden I have marigolds, candytuft, larkspur, and cornflowers.

(b) The five largest cities in Britain are London, Birmingham, Glasgow, Liverpool, and Manchester.

(c) Tennis, cricket, and swimming are my main pastimes in the summer.

(d) In his pocket he had three marbles, a piece of string, a French coin, a broken penknife, two boiled sweets, and a conker.

(e) Five gold rings, four calling birds, three French hens, two turtle doves, and a partridge in a pear tree.

(f) We had fish and chips, bread and butter, and a pot of tea.

PAGE 65

3. "You have not left enough space between COACH and AND, and AND and HORSES."

4. (a) Melt the butter in a saucepan, stir in the flour, add the fish stock, and stir until it thickens.

(b) Check the settings of the camera, make sure that your subject is correctly arranged in the viewfinder, hold your breath, and gently press the shutter-release.

(c) Wash cut-glass vases in warm soapy water, rinse well, dry with an old linen cloth, and polish with soft tissue-paper.

(d) Add the hot water to the dye, bring it to boiling-point, plunge the wet curtain into the dye-bath, and stir continually with a wooden rod.

(e) Fill the cracks with plaster of Paris, rub down with fine sandpaper, apply a coat of thin size, allow to dry, rub down again, and then apply the first coat of paint.

5. (a) Sir Humphry Davy, the inventor of the safety-lamp, died in 1829.

(b) Schubert, one of Germany's finest composers, wrote many beautiful melodies.

(c) John Bunyan, a travelling tinker, wrote *Pilgrim's Progress* in prison.

(d) The South Pole, a featureless spot in a wilderness of ice and snow, was first reached by Amundsen.

(e) The first English printer, William Caxton, was not actually the inventor of printing.

6. (a) However, at long last we reached the top of the hill.

(b) Indeed, there was enough food left for another good meal.

(c) In fact, I was too warm.

(d) For instance, we could do a charade.

(e) By the way, Rebel is my new pony.

(f) On the other hand, it may be that the letter never reached him.

7. (a) At long last, however, we reached the top of the hill.

(b) There was enough food left, indeed, for another good meal.

OR There was, indeed, enough food left for another good meal.

(c) I was, in fact, too warm.

(d) We could, for instance, do a charade.

(e) Rebel, by the way, is my new pony.

(f) It may be, on the other hand, that the letter never reached him.

PAGE 66

8. (a) (i) Wash your hands, Peter, and do your homework.

(ii) Wash your hands and do your homework, Peter.

(b) (i) I assure you, sir, that I am telling the truth.

(ii) I assure you that I am telling the truth, sir.

(c) (i) I have been wondering, Mother, if you would like a brooch for Christmas.

(ii) I have been wondering if you would like a brooch for Christmas, Mother.

(d) (i) I intend, ladies and gentlemen, to be as brief as I can.

(ii) I intend to be as brief as I can, ladies and gentlemen.

(e) (i) If you really want to play the piano, my dear boy, you must practise.

(ii) If you really want to play the piano you must practise, my dear boy.

9. (a) The second sentence means that all girls like knitting.

The first sentence means that those girls who like knitting will enjoy making the jumper.

(b) The first sentence means that golf is suitable for those men who like the open air.

The second sentence means that because all men like the open air many of them take up golf.

(c) (i) Paul
(ii) Donald

(d) The second sentence means that the man used his stick as a pointer.

The first sentence means that the man who showed us the way to go was the one with a walking-stick.

(e) The second sentence means that I had never flown at all before.

The first sentence means that I have just had my first glider-flight.

F. D. & C. Manual, p. 30

32. THE APOSTROPHE

1. has not   we have
   of the clock   though
   never   even
        Halloweven
   we will ⎫   cannot
   we shall ⎭   ever
   over   it was
   it is   did not

2. I'm   I've   I'd   I'll
   couldn't   you've   he'll   you're
   there's   it's   who's   who's
       where's   weren't

46

3. (a) Lord bless you.
   (b) All along the road.
   (c) Regular roughs.
   (d) Just as it was getting serious.
   (e) What do they do with them?
   (f) You would have laughed to see them.
   (g) He is an amazing fine runner.

4. (a) The grocer's shop
   (b) The grocers' shops
   (c) The farmer's fields
   (d) The farmers' fields
   (e) The pony's tail
   (f) The ponies' tails
   (g) The witch's broom
   (h) The witches' brooms

   F. D. & C. Manual, p. 26

5. (a) The surgery of the doctor
   (b) The lamps of the miners
   (c) The wings of the flies
   (d) The weapons of the pygmy
   (e) The parents of the princess
   (f) The father of the princesses
   (g) The nest of the wasps
   (h) The committee of ladies

6. (a) CHILDREN'S LIBRARY
   (b) BOYS' SCHOOL
   (c) MAYOR'S PARLOUR
   (d) WOMEN'S WARD
   (e) MEN'S OUTFITTER
   (f) LADIES' HAIRDRESSER
   (g) GIRLS' ENTRANCE
   (h) JONES'S STORES
   (i) PETS' CORNER
   (j) EMPLOYEES' CANTEEN

7. Cleopatra's Needle
   Queen Anne's Gate

Poets' Corner
St. Martin's in the Fields
Boy Scouts' Headquarters
People's Palace
All Souls' Church
St. James's Palace

8. LORRY'S BRAKES FAIL ON HILL
   TODAY'S SOCCER RESULTS
   FIRE DESTROYS NURSES' HOSTEL
   NEWS FROM ALL QUARTERS
   SHIP'S CREW ADRIFT IN BOATS
   CABINET MINISTERS AT ST. PAUL'S
   NEW ROUTES FOR LONDON BUSES
   PENSIONS FOR SOLDIERS' WIDOWS
   TWO MONTHS' RAIN IN THREE WEEKS
   ART GALLERIES' FINANCIAL DIFFICULTIES

33. QUOTATION-MARKS

1. (a) She looked at him and said, "You broke my window."
   (b) Father often says, "Make hay while the sun shines."
   (c) She paused for a few moments and then added, "Please forgive me."
   (d) I asked him if he was angry, and he answered, "Not really."
   (e) Leslie replied, "I think you've made a mistake."
   (f) I said, "Is there a theatre in this town?"

2. (a) "Today is my birthday," she said.
   (b) "I bought this in Venice," said Keith.
   (c) "This way, please," said one of the nurses.
   (d) "This is a new type of engine," he told me.

(e) "Are you being attended to?" asked the assistant.

(f) "Perhaps," mother said when I asked her if we were going to the seaside.

3. (a) "My lads," said Captain Smollett, "I've a word to say to you."

(b) "Well, Squire," said Dr. Livesey, "I don't put much faith in your discoveries."

(c) "Toss out the fire," said the Captain, "for we mustn't have smoke in our eyes."

(d) "If I see anyone," said Joyce, "am I to fire?"

(e) "One more step, Mr. Hands," said I, "and I'll blow your brains out."

(f) "John Silver," he said, "you're a prodigious villain and impostor."

4. (a) "This is my home," said the peasant. "I live here alone. You must not expect to find much comfort."

(b) "I was not asleep," replied the child. "The thunder has kept me awake. Please come and talk to me."

(c) "You surprise me," he answered. "I was talking to him only yesterday. Is he badly hurt?"

(d) "Are you angry?" she asked. "Have I offended you? I did not mean to hurt your feelings."

5. (a) 'The Invisible Man' was written by H. G. Wells.

(b) 'Curly' Stevens is a most amusing person.

(c) I am never sure of how to spell 'immediately'.

(d) He said that the 'cops' were looking for him.

(e) 'Corrections' is all you need write at the top of the page.

(f) John Fearn recited 'John Gilpin'.

(g) The description used on the application form is 'disabled persons'.

(h) The word before 'going' should be 'and'.

F. D. & C. Manual, p. 50

6. SUGGESTED ANSWERS

(a) "How old are you?"

(b) "If you break anything you will have to pay for it."

(c) "Do you feel hungry?"

(d) "I think I know where we are."

(e) "You must pay full price for him (her)."

F. D. & C. Manual, p. 42

PAGE 69

7. SUGGESTED ANSWERS

(a) Molly said that she had finished her examinations.

(b) Trevor said that the fire had gone out.

(c) The policeman told my uncle that he was not allowed to park his car there.

(d) Uncle John told me that when he was my age he had a pony of his own.

(e) I asked the conductor if that bus went to Piccadilly.

(f) Mr. Ward told her in reply that he thought she was being very selfish.

8. (a) The Mole said that it was all very well to talk.

(b) The Badger said that it was time they were all in bed.

(c) The Hedgehog replied that the master had gone into his study.

(d) The Rat said soothingly that he quite understood.

(e) The Mole told the Rat that he felt strangely tired.

(f) The girl told Toad to be quiet for a minute.

9. SUGGESTED ANSWERS

(a) The porter told me that the Bedford train had just gone.

(b) I asked him the time of the next one.

(c) He replied that there was a slow train at 10.15, but that I should not get a fast train until 1.45.

(d) I enquired if there was a refreshment room there.

(e) He answered that there was, and that I should find it on platform 3.

10.(a) "*I feel* honoured that *I have* been asked to distribute the prizes on *this* important occasion."

(b) "*We are* all glad that the weather *has* been so kind."

(c) "It *is* inevitable that some competitors *are* disappointed."

(d) "However, many records *have* been broken."

(e) "*I congratulate* those who *have* been successful."

(f) "*We shall* all look forward, *I am* sure, to meeting *here* again next year."

F. D. & C. Manual, p. 42

11.(a) *She was* delighted to be *there*.

(b) The people of Manbury *had* always made *her* welcome.

(c) There *was* no lovelier place in *that* county.

(d) The village green where *they were* gathered *had* been like *that* for centuries.

(e) *They* must be on *their* guard against those who *wished* to destroy it.

12.(a) *He had* been mayor of *that* town for three years.

(b) Many improvements *had* been carried out during *his* term of office.

(c) *They could* pride *themselves* on being progressive and enterprising.

(d) *He hoped* that *they would* continue to develop in *that* way.

(e) There *was* still much that *had* to be done.

(f) *He was* sure that *his* successor *could* count upon *their* full support.

PAGE 70

34. EXCLAMATION-MARKS

I. (a) What a tall man your father is!

(b) How stupid you are!

(c) How calm the lake is!

(d) What a nuisance it is!

(e) How pretty the bridesmaids look!

(f) What a pity it is that I missed you!

2. SUGGESTED ANSWERS

(a) Let me go!

(b) Be quick!

(c) Help!

(d) Be careful!

(e) Goal!

(f) Hold tight!

(g) Fire!

49

3. SUGGESTED ANSWERS

(a) He talks a lot of nonsense.
(b) You look very well.
(c) It is bitterly cold.
(d) We had a fierce gale last night.
(e) It is a great pity.
(f) He ran like the wind.

4. SUGGESTED ANSWERS

(a) If only my tooth would stop aching!
(b) If only Alan would lend me his racket!
(c) If only the sun would shine!
(d) If only I could remember Jim's address!
(e) If only I had worked harder!
(f) If only I were a little taller!
(g) If only I were old enough to drive a car!

5. (a) A fine cook you are!
(b) A pretty sight it looked!
(c) A great help that is!
(d) Much good that will do us!
(e) A lot of furniture you'll buy for ten pounds!
(f) A peaceful spot it was, with dogs barking all night!

6. What! Do you think we make no charge for admission?

35. HYPHENS

F. D. & C. Manual, p. 41

1. (a) scrap-ped, drag-ged, stun-ning, trot-ting, bud-ding, sham-ming.
(b) appear-ance, avoid-able, regret-ful, system-atic, peculiar-ity, knowingly.
(c) chang-ing, glid-ing, loung-ing, combin-ing, procur-ing, increasingly.
(d) crazi-ness, godli-ness, thrifti-est, thirsti-est, melodi-ously, reliability.

2. (a) A ten-kilometre race
(b) A hundred-pound bill
(c) An eight-day clock
(d) A two-litre kettle
(e) A ten-hectare field
(f) A half-kilogram weight
(g) An eight-page programme
(h) A four-door saloon
(i) A five-way junction
(j) A three-kilowatt fire
(k) An eighteen-hole golf-course
(l) A five-minute interval

3. (a) A top-heavy vase
(b) A red-hot poker
(c) An air-tight tin
(d) A bomb-proof shelter
(e) A thin-skinned orange
(f) A rough-haired dog
(g) An evil-smelling liquid
(h) A hard-working man
(i) A flat-footed person
(j) A prison-like building
(k) Under-done meat
(l) An over-valued house
(m) A high-spirited youth
(n) An evil-minded person

4. (a) Dancing-slippers
(b) A running-track

50

(c) A working-jacket
(d) A skipping-rope
(e) A jumping-pit
(f) A rocking-horse
(g) A smoking-concert
(h) A skating-rink
(i) A burning-glass
(j) Laughing-gas

5. (a) This is an *out-of-date* catalogue, and cannot be trusted.
   (b) Asleep on the seat was a *down-and-out* beggar.
   (c) Brian Mills gives an *on-the-spot* report in our next week's issue.
   (d) The *first-night* audience gave the play a good reception.
   (e) Ours has been a *long-standing* friendship.
   (f) It was a *never-to-be-forgotten* race.

PAGE 72
_____

6. (a) re-cover   (e) remark
   (b) recover   (f) re-sign
   (c) re-dress   (g) re-strain
   (d) resign   (h) recount

36. PARENTHESIS

1. (a) Several boys, none of whom I knew, walked over to us.
   (b) Now and then, as though dreaming, she smiled in her sleep.
   (c) I asked him, thinking that he was a policeman, which was the way to the library.
   (d) I have decided, having considered the situation very carefully, to postpone the event until next week.

(e) This book, though not the one I asked for, will do.
(f) Albert, however he tried, never managed to win a game.

2. (a) We rode on to the next village (Gamston) to see my aunt.
   (b) On the following day (Easter Monday) we went to Torquay.
   (c) Kenneth told Lionel that he (Lionel) had won a prize.
   (d) I took ten pence (all I had) from my purse and gave it to him.
   (e) A man was giving samples of chocolate (very small ones) to a queue of children.
   (f) My presents included a book, a pen, a torch (just the kind I wanted) and a pair of gloves.

   F. D. & C. Manual, p. 29

3. (a) Complete the coupon in ink—pencil will not do—and send it to the Editor.
   (b) I suggest that you go to Mr. Richards—remember to take your school report—and ask if he has a vacancy.
   (c) He searched the drawers—all the cupboards were locked—and found several photographs.
   (d) The great floods of 1953—nothing like them had been experienced for many years—caused widespread destruction.
   (e) Gloves—woollen ones are the best—should be grey or dark blue.
   (f) Of the three names that have been suggested for my baby brother—Roger, Gordon, and Gerald—I prefer Roger.

   F. D. & C. Manual, p. 35

37. SEMI-COLONS

1. (a) Football is a game for young men; many older men prefer golf.
   (b) Robins can sometimes be persuaded to come indoors, though this is not usual.
   (c) Cotton is a vegetable fibre; asbestos is a mineral.
   (d) Whereas linen is a natural fibre, nylon is artificial.
   (e) The inhabitants do not belong to the Christian faith; they are chiefly Hindus and Mohammedans.
   (f) Wise men learn by other men's mistakes; fools learn by their own.
   (g) As you make your bed, so you must lie on it.

2. (a) Cumulus clouds are heaped-up clouds; they look like piles of cotton wool.
   (b) These birds fly great distances; a journey of two hundred kilometres is nothing to them.
   (c) A mountain is made of harder rocks than its surroundings, and its shaping has been done mostly by running water.
   (d) The sun sets, night falls suddenly, and after the great heat of the day the desert becomes suddenly cold; this causes rocks to split and crumble.
   (e) The layers of tree-trunks and moss become more covered over with sand and mud, more compressed by the weight above them.
   (f) Like alligators, crocodiles lay eggs; snakes also reproduce themselves in this way.

★ REVISION

1. (a) BRITAIN'S LEAD IN EXPORTS
   (b) APPEAL TO DOCKERS' UNION
   (c) TWO MINISTERS SHARE FOREIGN AFFAIRS
   (d) PRINCE MEETS CRASH SURVIVORS
   (e) WOLVES' CHAMPIONSHIP HOPES
   (f) PRINCESS'S JEWELS STOLEN

2. (a) *All is* Well that Ends Well.
   (b) Like a worm *in* the bud.
   (c) And some have greatness thrust upon *them.*
   (d) O, what a noble mind is here *overthrown!*
   (e) Thou *knowest it is* common.
   (f) I *begin* to be aweary of the sun.
   (g) When my heart hath *escaped* this sorrow.
   (h) Home art gone, and *taken* thy wages.
   (i) His purse is empty already; *all his* golden words are spent.

3. (a) Joan of Arc inspired the French to drive the English out of Orleans.
   (b) When Napoleon had been defeated at Waterloo he was exiled to St. Helena.
   (c) Mary Queen of Scots was executed at Fotheringhay.
   (d) Sir Francis Drake, one of Queen Elizabeth's admirals, was largely responsible for the destruction of the Spanish Armada.
   (e) It was Sir Christopher Wren who reconstructed St. Paul's Cathedral after the Great Fire of London.

4. (a) What is the name of this village?
   (b) What a fine view this is!
   (c) I wonder where he went.

(*d*) How sharp is your pencil?
(*e*) How sharp your pencil is!
(*f*) Tell me how far it is to York.
(*g*) Can you tell me how far it is to York?
(*h*) Say how many people there are in the room.

PAGE 74

★ REVISION

1. (*a*) Five year-old children
   (*b*) Two litre paint tins
   (*c*) Forty odd people

2. (*b*) Gipsies who live in caravans are not often seen nowadays.

3. Sally is as tall as, if not taller than, Pamela.
   Sally is as tall as Pamela.

4. After they had finished their supper the woman cleared off the things and began to question the stranger.
   "Where are you from?"
   "I do not belong hereabouts."
   "How did you happen to get into this road?"
   "I cannot tell you."
   "Who maltreated you?"
   "God punished me."
   "And you were lying there stripped?"
   "Yes; there I was lying all naked, freezing to death, when Simon saw me, had compassion on me, took off his coat, put it on me, and bade me come home with him. You have fed me, given me something to eat and to drink, and have taken pity on me. May the Lord requite you!"

SECTION THREE
SPELLING

38. FIFTY TRICKY WORDS

recognize
separate
library
professor
campaign
literary
shepherd
parliament
luncheon
chocolate
unconscious
substantial
contemporary
cupboard
secondary
miniature
cemetery
maintenance
caterpillar
heretic
satellite
manœuvre
vacuum
raspberry
rhinoceros

propeller
diphtheria
auxiliary
labyrinth
diaphragm
terrestrial
pomegranate
mackerel
hygienic
mistletoe
mantelpiece
parallel
aspirin
laburnum
paraffin
rhododendron
veterinary
restaurant
sacrilegious
February
Portuguese
miscellaneous
exhaust
exhibition
buoyant

39. -ABLE AND -IBLE

(a) What makes him so *irritable*?

(b) This is a *sensible* suggestion.

(c) He would make an *admirable* prefect.

(d) Is the disease *curable*?

(e) Smoking is not *permissible* in this hall.

(f) Do you think it *advisable* for us to go without coats?

(g) The frost did a *negligible* amount of damage.

(h) Her stockings are almost *invisible*.

(i) Strong boots are *indispensable* for rock climbing.

(j) She is a very *excitable* girl.

(k) I hold you *responsible* for the safe keeping of this book.

(l) His insulting manner was *contemptible*.

(m) They told us an almost *incredible* story of hardship and danger.

(n) The village is not *approachable* from the north.

(o) The village is easily *accessible* from the west.

(p) Is it *practicable* for man to reach Mars?

54

40. DISAPPEARING LETTERS

(a) tigress
(b) humorous
(c) remembrance
(d) wondrous
(e) wintry
(f) proprietress
(g) encumbrance
(h) disastrous
(i) entrance
(j) humorist
(k) hindrance
(l) administration
(m) monstrous
(n) enchantress
(o) laborious
(p) vaporize
(q) carpentry
(r) generosity
(s) curiosity
(t) glamorous
(u) exclamation
(v) registrar
(w) repetition
(x) impetuosity
(y) pronunciation
(z) deodorant

41. SOME USEFUL ASSOCIATIONS

(a) The function of the *government* is to govern.
(b) A *terrific* explosion fills one with terror.
(c) A *secretary* may have to deal with secret documents.
(d) *Medicine* should be taken only on medical advice.
(e) A *cigarette* is a small cigar.
(f) Inflammation of the *bronchial* tubes is called bronchitis.
(g) A *balloon* is shaped like a large ball.
(h) *Christmas* is the festival of the birth of Christ.
(i) A birth *certificate* certifies the date of one's birth.
(j) We *commemorate* an event by keeping it in our memory.

42. -FUL, -FULLY

(a) A *playful* puppy
(b) A *plentiful* supply
(c) Sleeping *peacefully*
(d) A *joyful* occasion
(e) Yours *respectfully*
(f) A *fanciful* story
(g) *Beautifully* embroidered
(h) A *painful* sprain
(i) A *scornful* answer
(j) Treated *shamefully*
(k) *Pitifully* ill
(l) A lady *bountiful*

43. I BEFORE E

brief√	rein
priest √	veil
thief√	ceiling √
leisure	weight
height	shield √
deceive √	receipt √
believe√	pier√
piece √	conceit √

In all the underlined words the *ei* is preceded by *c*.

All the words not ticked contain *ei* preceded by a letter other than *c*.

NOTE: The rule is as follows:
When the diphthong rhymes with *bee*
The *i* must go before the *e*
Unless the diphthong follows *c*.

The words *leisure, height, rein, veil,* and *weight* are not exceptions to this rule, because in none of them does the *ei* rhyme with *bee*.

F. D. & C. Manual, p. 41

44. WORDS ENDING IN Y

factories supplies railways butterflies
abbeys jockeys dummies industries
collieries journeys ceremonies lorries
trolleys volleys colonies ferries
turkeys policies allies alleys
alloys ·beauties kidneys pygmies
melodies medleys laundries stories
storeys balconies decoys

2. (a) Have you *enjoyed* yourselves?
   (b) We were *delayed* by fog.
   (c) The story has been shortened and *simplified*.
   (d) I am *trying* to solve this puzzle.
   (e) And there I *espied* a fair pretty maid.
   (f) Three shops were *destroyed* by fire.
   (g) He was disqualified for not *obeying* the rules.
   (h) She is now *studying* biology.
   (i) The factory gives *employment* to many people.
   (j) They turned and *curtsied* to the queen.
   (k) The notices were prominently *displayed*.
   (l) Is my dog *annoying* you?
   (m) The land has not yet been *surveyed*.
   (n) They stood firm, *defying* all attempts to move them.
   (o) He bolted the door and *denied* us admission.

PAGE 78

45. DROPPING THE E

1. excitement   assurance
   amazing   lonely
   famous   spiteful

loving   idleness
excitable   amazement
senseless   separately
groping   separating
whitish   postponement

2. overtaking   traceable
   elopement   dining
   changeable   whiteness
   outrageous   peaceable
   desirable   nightmarish
   desirous   advantageous
   lately   observant
   latish   truly*
   manageable   noticeable

* Exception

46. HARD AND SOFT C AND G

(a) courageous (soft)
(b) catalogue (hard)
(c) noticeable (soft)
(d) gorgeous (soft)
(e) picnicked (hard)
(f) pigeon (soft)
(g) gracious (soft)
(h) peaceable (soft)
(i) plague (hard)
(j) manageable (soft)
(k) fatigue (hard)
(l) vengeance (soft)
(m) spacious (soft)
(n) changeable (soft)
(o) frolicked (hard)
(p) sergeant (soft)
(q) dialogue (hard)
(r) panicked (hard)
(s) serviceable (soft)
(t) surgeon (soft)
(u) outrageous (soft)
(v) vague (hard)

(w) pageant (soft)
(x) pronounceable (soft)
(y) mimicking (hard)
(z) intrigue (hard)

47. DOUBLING THE LAST LETTER

stepped, stepping
dropped, dropping
thinner, thinnest
hotter, hottest
sadder, saddest, sadness
reddest, reddish, redness
brimming, brimful
hatted, hatless
greeted, greeting
breakable, breaking
readable, reader
robbed, robber
sharpen, sharpest, sharply
sinner, sinning, sinful
bigger, biggest
hopped, hopping
fitted, fitness, fitment
flatten, flatter
dreaded, dreading, dreadful
greater, greatest, greatly

PAGE 79

48. DOUBLE L

labelled	wheeled
concealed	unveiling
prevailing	signalled
pedalling	revealed
toiled	panelled
travelling	retailed
patrolling	assailing
cooled	marshalling

quarrelling	curtailed
totalled	stencilling
pencilled	fouled
appealing	fulfilled
expelled	jewelled
feeling	unsealing
marvelled	shovelling
uncoiled	initialled*

*Or *initialed*; but the two vowels before the *l* do not give a long vowel-sound, so *initialled* is usually preferred.

49. DOUBLE T

1.
batting	rooted
petted	potted
greeting	netted
fitting	flirting
rotted	chatting
started	snorted
meeting	fretting
waited	jutting
strutting	pouted
knitting	spurting
cheated	quitted
suited	floating

2.
fidget	defeat
ballot	commit
pivot	submit
rivet	retort
budget	omit
trumpet	acquit
fillet	recruit
pocket	regret
profit	transmit
pilot	permit
ferret	await
benefit	outwit

fidgeted, fidgeting
balloted, balloting
pivoted, pivoting
riveted, riveting
budgeted, budgeting
trumpeted, trumpeting
filleted, filleting
pocketed, pocketing
profited, profiting
piloted, piloting
ferreted, ferreting
benefited, benefiting
defeated, defeating

committed, committing
submitted, submitting
retorted, retorting
omitted, omitting
acquitted, acquitting
recruited, recruiting
regretted, regretting
transmitted, transmitting
permitted, permitting
awaited, awaiting
outwitted, outwitting

PAGE 80

50. DOUBLE R

1. barred
   fearing
   cheered
   blurred
   whirring
   tarred
   wearing
   roared
   swearing
   starred

   moored
   paired
   stirring
   aired
   tearing
   slurred
   soared
   spurring
   sparring
   chaired

2. offer
   conquer
   enter
   motor
   suffer
   render
   pilfer

   occur
   incur
   refer
   repair
   prefer
   inter
   defer

differ
order
hinder
alter
labour

deter
forbear
bestir
debar
recur

offered, offering
conquered, conquering
entered, entering
motored, motoring
suffered, suffering
rendered, rendering
pilfered, pilfering
differed, differing
ordered, ordering
hindered, hindering
altered, altering
laboured, labouring

occurred, occurring
incurred, incurring
referred, referring
repaired, repairing
preferred, preferring
interred, interring
deferred, deferring
deterred, deterring
forbearing
bestirred, bestirring
debarred, debarring
recurred, recurring

51. DOUBLING BY PAIRING

1. dissatisfied, dissimilar
   unnecessary, unnatural, unnamed, unnumbered
   underrate, underrun
   overreach, overrule, overrun, override
   immortal, immature, immeasurable, immoral, immovable, immodest

2. greenness   soulless   wheelless
   keenness   thinness   tailless
   drunkenness soilless   suddenness
   plainness   oilless   veilless
   goalless

58

WORD STUDY

52. VOWELS AND CONSONANTS

1. mathematics, composition, needle-work, woodwork, geometry, history, typewriting, scripture.

ftbll	hcky	bdmntn	bllrds
rndrs	sktng	sqsh	

2. knife   comb   gnat   honest
   wrinkle listen island solemn
   salmon   psalm   reign   weight

3. (a) board, fall, maul, fought
   (b) fruit, rude, rue, shoe, you, soon
   (c) wheel, seize, yield, feast
   (d) veil, gaol, fate, great, pain, fête

4. (a) hoe, float, sold
   (b) aisle, find, choir, height, lie
   (c) mend, any, friend, leisure, said, bury, head, leopard
   (d) hunt, rough, blood, son

5. (a) knit   (f) banana
   (b) lamb   (g) football
   (c) gaiety   (h) freedom
   (d) searchlight (i) ragged
   (e) try

6. (a) long   (i) long
   (b) short   (j) short
   (c) short   (k) short
   (d) long   (l) long
   (e) short   (m) short
   (f) long   (n) long
   (g) long   (o) long
   (h) short   (p) short

7. Oral exercise.

8. an uncle   a uniform
   an umbrella   an undergraduate
   a unicorn   a utensil
   an umpire   a university
   a ukulele   a union
   an upheaval   an ultimatum

9. a daring escape
   an idle scamp
   a hard-working boy
   an hourly service
   an unusual shape
   a usual custom
   a remote ancestor
   an icy wind
   a handsome man
   a useful tool
   an obvious mistake
   an unwise remark
   a tall iris
   an even keel
   an honourable agreement

a unique occasion
an unexpected event
an antique chest
a horrible expression
a diesel engine
an ugly house
an open door
a large orchard
a unison song
an endless belt
a triumphal arch
an accurate timekeeper
an uphill climb
a unanimous decision
an honorary secretary

53. SYLLABLES

1. sub-tract   en-er-get-ic
con-demn   com-part-ment
mag-net-ic   dis-con-tent-ment
pub-lish-ing   tel-e-graph
re-lent-less   ro-ta-tion

2. tomato (3)
invent (2)
encyclopedia (6)
explorer (3)
revolution (4)
octave (2)
impatiently (4)
modern (2)
jamboree (3)
film (1)
straight (1)
fortunate (3)
war (1)
umbrella (3)
locomotive (4)
misunderstanding (5)

complimentary (5)
unintelligently (6)
discontentedly (5)
systematically (6)
intercommunication (7)

3. SUGGESTED ANSWERS

(a) old
(b) quick, fast, swift
(c) small, dwarf
(d) huge, great
(e) brave, grand, fine
(f) dark, dim, dull
(g) hard
(h) gay, blithe
(i) high, tall
(j) weak, frail
(k) bad, base, vile
(l) wrong, false
(m) sad
(n) rough

4. Free composition.

5. commanded, created, fulfilling, excellent, exalteth, Israel

6. SUGGESTED ANSWERS

(a) daring, dauntless, fearless, gallant, plucky
(b) surprised, amazed
(c) bashful, timid, modest
(d) brilliant, glittering, luminous, radiant
(e) curious, perplexing, surprising
(f) terrified, faint-hearted
(g) diminutive, Lilliputian, microscopic, miniature
(h) incapable, incompetent, inefficient
(i) contaminated
(j) infuriated

(k) disagreeable, uncomfortable, un-
desirable
(l) disreputable

54. PRONUNCIATION

F. D. & C. Manual, p. 134

1.

First	*Second*
daughter	repose
bushes	divide
slumber	asleep
dreaming	forget
woven	unfurled
midnight	farewell
garland	awake
silence	complete
broken	proclaim
mountains	deceive
lightning	withdrawn
morning	obey

2.

First	*Second*	*Third*
innocent	reflection	discontent
melody	immortal	violin
universe	eternal	understand
nightingale	triumphant	interrupt
galloping	remembrance	disappear
sorrowful	devotion	overhead
weariness	forgetful	mutineer
festival	reluctant	reunite

PAGE 84

3.
(a) Two; 1st.
(b) Two; 2nd.
(c) Three; 2nd.
(d) Two; 1st,
(e) Three; 1st.
(f) Two; 2nd.
(g) Three; 2nd.
(h) Two; 1st.
(i) Three; 1st.
(j) Three; 2nd.
(k) Three; 1st.
(l) Two; 1st.
(m) Two; 2nd.
(n) Three; 2nd.
(o) Four; 2nd.
(p) Two; 2nd.
(q) Three; 1st.
(r) Four; 1st.
(s) Two; 2nd.
(t) Five; 2nd.

4.
(a) ear-wig
(b) ex-plain
(c) em-ploy-ment
(d) fault-less-ly
(e) doc-tor
(f) dis-con-tin-ue
(g) gym-nas-tic
(h) dis-gust
(i) hipp-o-pot-a-mus
(j) pho-to-graph
(k) pho-tog-raph-y
(l) pho-to-graph-ic

5.
(a) mid'land
(b) estab'lishment
(c) enjoy'
(d) lo'comotive*
(e) frank'incense
(f) event'ful
(g) repeat'
(h) personal'ity
(i) perform'
(j) a'corn
(k) o'vercoat
(l) overflow'ing

*or locomo'tive

6.
(a) Noun; rec'ord.
(b) Verb: suspect'.
(c) Verb; transport'.
(d) Noun; con'duct.
(e) Noun; prod'uce.
(f) Verb; transfer'.
(g) Noun; ref'use.
(h) Verb; convict'.

F. D. & C. Manual, p. 23

7.
im'potent	in'famous
for'midable	gon'dola
in'ventory	catas'trophe
rep'utable	super'fluous
flaming'o	incom'parable
lam'entable	ve'hement

8.

Hard	*Soft*
local	cellar
concrete	hyacinth
correct	city
script	recipe

61

Hard	Soft
calico	incense
piccolo	façade

9.

Hard	Soft	Silent
grind	gesticulate	reign
dagger	general	gnaw
pilgrim	sergeant	poignant
golliwog	longitude	gnat
disgusting	orgy	gnash
giggle	magic	gnarled
	pageant	
	gesture	

F. D. & C. Manual, p. 40

PAGE 85

---

10. overhang   hollyhock   headlight
cloth   thigh   wholesome
honesty   haphazard   hourly
when   shorthand   withhold

11. The given words are repeated here for the convenience of the teacher.

  (*a*) h in *heir*   (*g*) s in *débris*
  (*b*) ps in *corps*   (*h*) g in *gnarled*
  (*c*) b in *subtle*   (*i*) p in *pneumatic*
  (*d*) g in *feign*   (*j*) h in *thyme*
  (*e*) t in *sabot*   (*k*) w in *gunwale*
  (*f*) b in *debtor*   (*l*) g in *poignant*

12. tĭmber   sōcial   pĕnny   dīver
āpricot   mŏnarch   būgle   băttery
bŭngalow   prēhistoric

13. băde   hŏver   păgeant   vĭneyard
glăcier   crōchet   līchen   tornādo
pūny   zēbra   tōpaz   grātis
cōbra   bābel   dīnosaur   recūperate
vacūŭm   dĕpōt

14. The given words and letters are repeated here for the convenience of the teacher.

  (*a*) *au* in *mauve* = ō
  (*b*) *er* in *clerk* = ar
  (*c*) *o* in *cobalt* = ō
  (*d*) *ch* in *orchid* = k
  (*e*) *et* in *crochet* = ā
  (*f*) *æ* in *phœnix* = ē
  (*g*) *is* in *viscount* = ı
  (*h*) *ai* in *plait* = ă
  (*i*) *er* in *sergeant* = ar
  (*j*) *eau* in *plateau* = ō
  (*k*) *i* in *fatigue* = ē
  (*l*) *ot* in *depot* = ō
  (*m*) *ch* in *chateau* = sh
  (*n*) *a* in *scallop* = ŏ
  (*o*) *ê* in *fête* = ā
  (*p*) *i* in *physique* = ē
  (*q*) *ui* in *sluice* = oo
  (*r*) *g* in *orgy* = j
  (*s*) *g* in *longitude* = j
  (*t*) *ch* in *architect* = k
  (*u*) the middle letter of *suede* = ā

15.   (*a*) ăc′robăt   (*g*) pŏpūlā′tion
        (*b*) ĭnhăb′ĭt   (*h*) ĭn′sūlāte
        (*c*) rĭdĭc′ūlous   (*i*) hū′man
        (*d*) commĕnce′   (*j*) hūmāne′
        (*e*) īdĕn′tĭcal   (*k*) rhōdodĕn′dron
        (*f*) lăt′ĭtūde   (*l*) commō′tion

55. PREFIXES AND SUFFIXES

1.   (*a*) un-employ-ment
     (*b*) un-pleasant-ness
     (*c*) im-prison-ment
     (*d*) dis-appear-ance
     (*e*) un-certain-ty

(f) re-appear-ing
(g) in-definite-ly
(h) re-construct-ion
(i) mis-understand-ing
(j) ir-regular-ly
(k) in-formal-ly
(l) in-accurate-ly
(m) dis-honour-able
(n) dis-respect-ful

F. D. & C. Manual, p. 36

2. The prefix is *dis-*. There is no double *s* unless the word to which *dis-* is prefixed begins with *s* — as in *dissatisfied*.

3. (a) I am *uncertain* about the date.
   (b) Destroy any copies that are *imperfect*.
   (c) His attendance is *irregular*.
   (d) These are *inexpensive* handbags.
   (e) Be careful not to do anything that is *illegal*.
   (f) That sounds an *improbable* story.
   (g) Have I called at an *inconvenient* time?
   (h) Good team-work calls for *unselfish* co-operation.
   (i) The stone slab was *immovable*.
   (j) My future plans are *undecided*.
   (k) This tape-measure is *inaccurate*.
   (l) The vicar reproved them for their *irreverent* behaviour.

4. SUGGESTED ANSWERS

   (a) not possible
   (b) chief bishop
   (c) not mortal
   (d) half sphere
   (e) in front of the head
   (f) not curable
   (g) in place of the president

(h) self-mobile
(i) not natural
(j) across the Atlantic
(k) not responsible
(l) half-circle
(m) against septic (or sepsis)
(n) not legible

5. SUGGESTED ANSWERS

   (a) to use wrongly
   (b) to join again
   (c) to tell beforehand
   (d) a way under
   (e) to capture again
   (f) going before
   (g) woven between
   (h) to judge beforehand

6. (a) secondary   (g) infirmary
   (b) imaginary   (h) legendary
   (c) observatory   (i) drudgery
   (d) embroidery   (j) dispensary
   (e) stationery   (k) migratory
   (f) preparatory   (l) monastery

7. (a) assistant   (e) excellent
   (b) resident   (f) ignorant
   (c) buoyant   (g) obedient
   (d) vigilant   (h) abundant

PAGE 87

8. (a) appearance   (d) existence
   (b) reverence   (e) assurance
   (c) condolence   (f) abstinence

9. (a) darkness   (g) bondage
   (b) ownership   (h) knighthood
   (c) childhood   (i) patriotism
   (d) cowardice   (j) shrinkage
   (e) heroism   (k) weariness
   (f) fellowship   (l) service

63

(a) feverish
(b) dangerous
(c) sinful, sinless
(d) heroic
(e) fearful, fearless
(f) woody, wooden
(g) dusty, dustless
(h) warlike
(i) hatless
(j) magnetic
(k) saintly, saintlike
(l) flaxen
(m) kingly, kingless, kinglike
(n) godly, godless, godlike
(o) glorious
(p) sunny, sunless, sunlike
(q) plentiful, plenteous
(r) stony, stoneless
(s) stylish
(t) volcanic

11.(a) booklet   (f) duckling
   (b) kitchenette   (g) maisonette
   (c) hillock   (h) granule
   (d) lancet   (i) globule
   (e) statuette   (j) gosling

F. D. & C. Manual, p. 36

PAGE 88

56. STORIES ABOUT WORDS

1. gypsies, gipsies
2. A shore
3. Because he fought with a sword
4. salary
5. navvy
6. journey, journal
7. (a) Put it on   (c) Do off
   (b) Take it off   (d) Do out
8. canter
9. breakfast
10. A mad-house, or uproar and confusion
11. (a) halibut
    (b) holidays
12. handicap

PAGE 89

13. (a) An artificial and decorated cave
    (b) grotesque
14. furlong
15. It had a winding course.
16. ironmonger
    costermonger
17. vaccination
18. scapegoat; a person who is blamed for the faults of others
19. panic
20. laconic
21. (a) carnival
    (b) carnation, carnivorous
    (c) Embodied in flesh; existing in human form
22. tawdry; showy, but cheap and common
23. vocation
24. (a) apron, adder, newt
    In *napron* and *naddre* the initial *n* has been transferred to *a* to make *an*. The word *ewt* has become *newt* by transference of the *n* from *an*.
    (b) Nickname
25. *Nausea* is a feeling of sickness such as sea-sickness; *nautical* means 'concerning sailors and ships.'
26. galaxy; a splendid gathering
27. (a) calcium
    (b) calculate
    chalk
28. supercilious

57. WORDS FROM OLD ENGLISH

(a) bucket   (f) drift
(b) hamlet   (g) fret
(c) husband   (h) bitter
(d) seldom   (i) settle
(e) bereave   (j) steadfast

58. NEAR RELATIONS

SUGGESTED ANSWERS

(1) dignity, dignified, dignitary
(2) appeal, appellant, appellation
(3) chamber. (Note *chamberlain*.)
(4) mortal, mortify, mortuary
(5) couch. (Note *couchant*.)
(6) facilitate, facility. (Note *faculty*.)
(7) comprehend
(8) chant, chantry. (Note *chanty*.)
(9) temporary, temporal, temporize
(10) language
(11) utilize, utility
(12) coffer, coffin
(13) celestial
(14) terminate, terminus, terminal. (Note *term*.)
(15) rouge
(16) portal, portcullis, porter (door-keeper), portico. (Note *port*.)
(17) tardy
(18) malady. (Note *malaise, malignant*.)
(19) pendant, pendulum, pendulous. (Note *pending*.)
(20) dormant, dormitory, dormouse
(21) pensive
(22) chandelier, chandler
(23) brunette
(24) cygnet
(25) escalator
(26) annual, anniversary, annuity. (Note *annals*.)
(27) ornament, ornate
(28) aviation, aviator
(29) liberty, liberate, liberal
(30) female, feminine
(31) solar. (Note *solarium*.)
(32) lunar. (Note *lunatic*.)
(33) territory, terrestrial, terrain. (Note *terrace, terrier*.)
(34) luminous, luminary
(35) petty. (Note *petticoat, pettifogging*.)
(36) donation, donor
(37) veritable, verify, veracious. (Note *very, verily, verdict*.)
(38) vine, vineyard, vintage, vintner. (Note *vinegar*.)
(39) arboreal, arbour, arboretum
(40) lavatory, lave
(41) jaundice
(42) vend, vendor or vender
(43) nominate, nominal, nomenclature
(44) matins or mattins. (Note *matinée, matutinal*.)
(45) amiable, amicable, amity
(46) blanch, blancmange, blank
(47) pontoon
(48) mural. (Note *murage*.)
(49) parley, parliament, parlance. (Note *parlour*.)
(50) filament, fillet, filigree. (Note *file*.)

59. WORDS FROM THE LATIN

I. SUGGESTED ANSWERS

(a) aviary, aviation, aviator
(b) gradation, grade, gradual
(c) grateful, gratitude, gratify
(d) vest, vestment, vestry
(e) linen. (Note *line, linseed, linnet, lint, linoleum*.)

(f) tremble, tremor, tremulous. (Note *tremendous*.)
(g) famine, famish
(h) barber, barb, barbel
(i) local, locate. (Note *locomotive, locus*.)
(j) alternate, alternative, alteration. (Note *altercation*.)
(k) rotate, rotary, rotor. (Note *rotund*.)
(l) vagabond, vagrant. (Note *vague, vagary*.)
(m) fraternal, fraternity, fraternize. (Note *fratricide*.)
(n) sanctify, sanctity, sanctuary, sanctimonious. (Note *sanction*.)
(o) filament, fillet, filigree. (Note *file*.)
(p) veritable, verify, veracious. (Note *very, verily, verdict*.)
(q) augment
(r) festival, festive, festivity, festal. (Note *festoon*.)
(s) durable. (Note *duress, durance, duration*.)
(t) grain, granary, granulated. (Note *grange, granite*.)
(u) err, errant, erratic, error, erroneous.
(v) canine. (Note *canary*.)
(w) feline
(x) floral, floret, florist, floriculture. (Note *florid, flourish*.)

PAGE 91

2. SUGGESTED ANSWERS

(a) incredible, incredulous
(b) infidel, infidelity
(c) portfolio
(d) co-operate
(e) refrigerator
(f) contribute, distribute
(g) enumerate, innumerable

(h) inanimate
(i) erupt, interrupt
(j) eradicate
(k) emigrate, immigrate
(l) corrode

📖 LOOK THESE UP

1. (a) There were no striking clocks in Caesar's day.
   (b) Nylon was not introduced until about 250 years after the reign of Charles II.

2. We are in effect repeating the phrase *of stars*, because the collective noun *constellation* means *a group of stars*; an example of redundancy.

3. (a) First person singular
   (b) Third person singular
   (c) Third person plural
   (d) First person plural
   (e) Third person singular

4. tinkle, clatter, quack

5. A metaphor.

Revision (Illustrated exercise)

(1) A *gypsy* (or *gipsy*) is one of those people who were thought to have come from *Egypt*.
(2) The *gladiolus* has a leaf shaped like a *sword* (L. *gladius*).
(3) To *canter* is to go at a *Canterbury* gallop.
(4) The time of *carnival* was a prelude to the "putting away of *flesh*".

66

60. FIND THE ROOT

(1) centurion
(2) pedal
(3) dictate
(4) clamour
(5) novelty
(6) dental
(7) aquarium
(8) octopus

(9) pacify
(10) malice
(11) patriarch
(12) final
(13) biology
(14) petrify
(15) corporation
(16) corps

(17) novice
(18) junction
(19) cavity
(20) primer
(21) fluent

(22) malady
(23) quadrilaterals
(24) chronicle
(25) decade

Other exercises of this pattern are given on page 201 of *A First English Companion*.

F. D. & C. Manual, p. 39

61. WORDS WITH TWO ROOTS

(a) microphone
(b) unison
(c) philanthropist
(d) barometer

(e) megaphone
(f) manufacture
(g) revoke

Other exercises of this pattern are given on pages 208 and 216 of *A First English Companion*.

62. FIND THE WORDS

(a) pedestal
(b) quadrangle
(c) monocle

(d) biped
(e) photograph
(f) trident

63. WORD FAMILIES

I. (a) triangle
   (b) tripod, tricycle
   (c) triplets, trio
   (d) tricolour
   (e) Trinity

2. (a) captain
   (b) capital
   (c) capital
   (d) cape
   (e) To cut off the head

3. portfolio, portmanteau, portable, porter

4. (a) audience, auditorium, audible
   (b) audition
   (c) Too faint to be heard.

5. (1) century
   (2) cent
   (3) centenarian
   (4) centurion
   (5) centigrade
   (6) centenary

6. duet, duel, dual or double, duplicate

7. (a) fortified, fort or fortress, fortitude
   (b) The use of strength; to make more strong, or to give added strength

8. (a) puppet
   (b) puppy
   (c) pupa

9. (a) puncture
   (b) punctuation
   (c) punctual

10. (a) terrace
    (b) territory
    (c) terrier
    (d) terrestrial
    (e) To bury in the earth.

II. (a) vista
    (b) vision

67

(c) visualize
(d) Not able to be seen. To see that work is properly done. Easily seen or understood.

12. vital, vitamins, vitality

13. (a) granary, grange
(b) granite
(c) pomegranate

14. (a) solo, sole
(b) solitary, solitude
(c) Left alone.

15. (a) philosopher, philanthropist
(b) Loving harmony or music.
(c) Lover of horses.

16. (a) tractor, traction
(b) To draw towards.
To draw out forcibly.
To draw back.
To draw away one's attention.
To draw out to a greater length.

17. (a) pork
(b) porcupine
(c) porcelain

18. (a) magnate, magnificent
(b) magnify, magnitude

19. (a) crucified, crucifix, crusades
(b) In the form of a cross.
(c) Very severe pain is said to be *excruciating* because it resembles the torture of being nailed to a cross.
To *cruise* is to *cross* the sea.

20. (a) In a monastery.
(b) A monarch.

(c) monotonous
(d) A monogram.
(e) A monopoly.
(f) A speech given by one person alone.
A word of one syllable alone.

21. (a) scribes, script, scripture
(b) To write or engrave on.
An account of something in writing.
To copy out in writing.
A doctor's written order for a certain medicine.

22. (a) temporary, temporal
(b) Belonging to the same period of time.

23. (a) spectacle, spectators
(b) specimen
(c) The spectrum.
(d) To look forward to.
To look at closely.
To honour or look up to.
Something to look at, or to look forward to; to look for (gold, etc.).

24. (a) manuscript   (d) manipulation
(b) manicure   (e) management
(c) manacle

25. (a) amble   (c) perambulator
(b) ambulance   (d) somnambulist

Revision (Illustrated exercise)

(1) *Panic* is the kind of fear that is supposed to have been caused by the god *Pan*.

68

(2) A *handicap* is the kind of forfeit or penalty that was imposed in the game of *hand in the cap* (*hand i' cap*).

(3) The *navvy* employed in the digging of 'navigations' (canals) was known as a *navigator*.

(4) *Vaccination* involves inoculation with a preparation derived from the *cow* (L. *vacca*).

PAGE 97

64. WORDS FROM MANY LANGUAGES

kaolin [Chin.]	cigar [Sp.]
bazaar [Pers.]	Hallelujah [Heb.]
mammoth [Russ.]	jungle [Hind.]
bandit [It.]	poodle [G.]
trek [Du.]	ranch [Sp.]
sofa [Arab.]	sonata [It.]
loot [Hind.]	jackal [Pers.]
sago [Malay]	tank [Port.]
bungalow [Hind.]	waltz [G.]
cockatoo [Malay]	yacht [Du.]
tea [Chin.]	pampas [Peruv.]
garage [Fr.]	caravan [Pers.]
lingerie [Fr.]	geyser [Icel.]
steppe [Russ.]	lama [Tibetan]
seraph [Heb.]	trousseau [Fr.]
balcony [It.]	molasses [Port.]

65. SOME INTERESTING DERIVATIONS

(a) Malaya; man of the woods.
(b) shade
(c) fourteen nights
(d) small
(e) *el lagarto*, the lizard
(f) almost island
(g) orphaned or bereft
(h) Paper of a certain size; it used to bear a watermark representing a jester's cap.
(i) thousand
(j) empty tomb; on a tomb
(k) Because *kindergarten* means *children's garden.*
(l) Because it is brought in after the table has been cleared.
(m) terrible lizard
(n) simpleton or silly
(o) It is derived from a word that means *mosquito-net.*
(p) at length
(q) *Blancmange* means *white food.*
(r) fifth essence

PAGE 98

66. PLACES AND PEOPLE

(1) Milan.
(2) From the name of the botanist *Magnol.*
(3) It was a Spanish dog, and derived its name from the words *español* (Spanish), *espaigneul.*
(4) Because italic type originated in *Italy.*
(5) The first mausoleum was the tomb of king *Mausolus.*
(6) In the French province of *Artois.*
(7) The French scientist *Pasteur.*
(8) Because the man who introduced tobacco into France was named *Nicot.*
(9) Ceres.
(10) Magnesia.

See also pages 160–1 of *A First English Companion.*

67. SOME APT COMPARISONS

(1) *Cirrus* cloud is light and fleecy like a *curl*.
(2) The function of a *molar* is to grind like a *millstone*.
(3) A *comet* seems to have long *hair* trailing behind it.
(4) The *daisy*, which opens in the morning, derives its name from the words *day's eye*.
(5) *Khaki* cloth was chosen for soldiers' uniforms because it was so much like the *dust* of the desert that it was a good camouflage.
(6) Some of the fat used in the making of *margarine* forms into glistening drops that look like *pearls*.
(7) The word *muscle* comes from a Latin word meaning *little mouse*.
(8) A *stimulus* acts as a *goad* to prod a person into being more active.

PAGE 99

68. LOOKING BACK

(1) God be with you! (Often written *God b'w'y*.)
(2) Forty days
(3) By mounting on a bench.
(4) near dweller (farmer, peasant)
(5) Moorish dancing
(6) moon
(7) grandfather (or godfather)
(8) A roll
(9) A woman who spins
(10) *piano e forte* or *pianoforte*; soft and strong.
(11) In the phrase *an orange* the indefinite article has gained an *n* at the expense of the Arabic word *naranj* or the old French word *narange*—that is, *a narange* has become *an orange*. In the phrase *a notch* the indefinite article has lost an *n* to the French word *hoche* (a nick in a tally); that is, *an hoche* has become *a notch*.
(12) The three divisions of Yorkshire were originally known as *thrithings* or *thridings* (i.e., third parts). The *th* of *north* and the *th* of *thriding* have coalesced to give us *North Riding*.

69. ADOPTED WORDS

(1) A defendant who says that he has an *alibi* claims to have been *elsewhere* when the offence was committed.
(2) A *souvenir* helps one to *remember* a past occasion.
(3) An *omnibus* (now called a *bus*) is a vehicle *for all*.
(4) Strictly speaking, a *café* is a place where *coffee* is served.
(5) An *opera* is a dramatic *work* in which music is an essential part.
(6) A *nebula* is a patch of light in the sky that looks like *mist*.
(7) *Neon* gas was so named because it was a *new* gas.
(8) When a governor decides to *veto* a suggestion he says, "*I forbid* it".
(9) When a judge issues a *fiat* he is in effect saying, "*Let it be done*".
(10) The noun 'table' is of *neuter* gender because it belongs to *neither* gender.
(11) A singer is given an *encore* when the audience wishes to hear him *again*.
(12) The *focus* of a living-room on a winter's night is the *hearth*.
(13) An *ignoramus* and his stupid companions are likely to answer many

questions by saying, "*We do not know*".

(14) During the *Renaissance*, interest in the arts and in learning was *born again*.

(15) "Hull *via* York" means "Hull by *way* of York".

(16) A *piccolo* is a *small* flute.

(17) In the earliest kind of *camera*, pictures were made by light in a dark room or *vault* (or *chamber*).

(18) A tableau is a group of persons arranged so as to form a *picture*.

(19) A bride's *trousseau* was originally a *bundle* of clothes, etc.

70. FIND THE LINK

(1) Latin *cloca*, bell
(2) Latin *plenus*, full
(3) Latin *altus*, high
(4) Latin *dorsum*, back
(5) Latin *folium*, leaf
(6) Latin *ligare*, bind
(7) Latin *cumulus*, heap
(8) Latin *colare*, strain
(9) Latin *cornu*, horn
(10) Greek *kalos*, beautiful
(11) Latin *mirari*, wonder at
(12) Latin *torquere*, twist
(13) Latin *grex, gregis*, flock
(14) Latin *scintilla*, spark
(15) Latin *acer*,
Old French *aigre*,} keen, sour
(16) Latin *pilus* and *capillus*, hair
(17) Latin *juvenis*, young
(18) Latin *panis*, bread
(19) Latin *nox, noctis*, night

(20) Latin *candidus*, white
candere, be white
(21) Latin *turba*, crowd, tumult
(22) Latin *caper*, goat
(23) Latin *malleus*, hammer
(24) Latin *lapis*, stone
(25) Latin *cancelli*, cross-bars or lattice-bars

F. D. & C. Manual, pp. 58–61

71. WORD CHAINS

(a)	(d)
benediction	intersect
malediction	bisect
malevolent	biennial
benevolent	triennial
benefactor	triplicate
malefactor	quadruplicate
	quadruped
(b)	centipede
stereoscope	centimetre
microscope	perimeter
micrometer	periscope
chronometer	telescope
chronology	telephone
astrology	megaphone
astronomy	megalith
autonomy	monolith
	monologue
(c)	biology
magnanimous	biography
unanimous	photography
unilateral	photometer
multilateral	geometry
multiplication	geography
duplication	autograph

71

(1) puppet, puppy, pupa.   They are derived from the Latin word meaning *a doll*.

(2) crusade, crucifix, cruciform; from the Latin word meaning *a cross*.

(3) ambulance, perambulator, somnambulist; from the Latin word meaning *to walk*.

Word Families (Illustrated exercise)

(1) tricycle, tripod, trio. They are derived from the Greek or Latin prefix meaning *three*.

(2) manicure, manuscript, manacle; from the Latin word meaning *the hand*.

(3) duet, duel, duplicate; from the Latin word meaning *two*.

SOME MISTAKES TO AVOID

The words to be used in Sets 72–75 can be found by the pupil, alphabetically arranged and with explanations of their meanings, in *A First English Companion*.

PAGE 103

72. SOME BAD MISTAKES

1. (a) If you run after *two* hares you will catch neither.
   (b) Eat *to* live, but do not live *to* eat.
   (c) *Two* eyes can see more than one.
   (d) It is *too* late *to* grieve when the chance is past.
   (e) It takes *two to* make a quarrel.

2. (a) Lookers-on see most *of* the game.
   (b) Never put *off* till tomorrow what may be done today.
   (c) Two dogs fight for a bone, and a third runs *off* with it.
   (d) A man *of* words and not *of* deeds is like a garden full *of* weeds.
   (e) Better a finger *off* than always aching.

3. (a) Go *there* on your way home.
   (b) They went with *their* parents.
   (c) *There* are ink-stains on *their* clothes.
   (d) *Their* luggage was *there* before them.
   (e) They handed in *their* papers to *their* teachers.

   F. D. & C. Manual, p. 55

4. (a) *It's* my birthday today.
   (b) This tree is shedding *its* leaves.
   (c) When *it's* melted *it's* ready to use.
   (d) *Its* breadth is half *its* length.
   (e) *It's* possible that the spice has lost *its* flavour.

5. (a) The green towels are *theirs*, not ours.
   (b) I shall cover the stool as well, if *there's* enough material.
   (c) *There's* less than half a loaf left.
   (d) These are your sandwiches on the table; Paul and David have taken *theirs*.
   (e) *Theirs* was the only yacht to finish the course.

PAGE 104

6. (a) *Who's* been eating my porridge?
   (b) *Whose* slippers are these?
   (c) This is the girl *whose* purse you found.
   (d) Go and see *who's* knocking.
   (e) He was a man *whose* only hobby was reading.

7. (a) Mary wants to *learn* shorthand, but can find no-one to *teach* her.

73

(b) Please *teach* me to knit; I am anxious to *learn*.

(c) Boy Scouts are *taught* to be kind and helpful to others.

(d) Until you have *learned* how to do something yourself you should not try to *teach* others.

(e) Last year Mr. Murray *taught* Peter to play the violin; he said that Peter *learned* very quickly.

8. (a) May I *borrow* your pencil, please?

(b) Brenda has lost her rubber; may she *borrow* yours?

(c) David may *borrow* my bat if he will *lend* me his fishing-rod.

(d) If you *borrow* money you may not be able to repay it.

(e) If you *lend* money you may not be able to get it back.

73. NOUN OR VERB?

1. (a) Are we allowed to *practise* running in the park?

(b) We have a rugger *practice* to-morrow.

(c) *Practice* makes perfect.

(d) *Practise* what you preach.

(e) You must *practise* regularly; an hour's *practice* a day is the least you should do.

2. (a) Must I have a *licence* for my puppy?

(b) What will it cost to *license* him?

(c) They refused to *license* the shop for the sale of spirits.

(d) My television-*licence* expires next week.

(e) You must *license* the car if you mean to take it out, but no *licence*

is needed while you keep it in the garage.

3. (a) What do you *advise* me to do?

(b) What *advice* did you give him?

(c) I *advise* you to get expert *advice*.

(d) He likes to *advise* others, but seldom follows his own *advice*.

(e) They may *advise* you to learn Spanish, but I *advise* you to take French.

4. (a) For we know in part, and we *prophesy* in part.

(b) Blessed are they that hear the words of this *prophecy*.

(c) And in them is fulfilled the *prophecy* of Esaias.

(d) And he pronounced this *prophecy* against me.

(e) He doth not *prophesy* good concerning me.

74. SOME FINER POINTS

1. (a) *Besides* hockey she plays netball and tennis.

(b) This wool is too thick; *besides*, it is the wrong colour.

(c) *Beside* the palace gate stood a sentry.

(d) The dog waited patiently *beside* his master.

(e) I have other hobbies *besides* painting.

2. (a) The bull charged to and fro *among* the spectators.

(b) They wondered what use five loaves and two fishes could be *among* five thousand people.

(c) The housework can be shared *between* the two of us.

(d) The votes were evenly divided *between* Mr. Lees and Mr. Horton.

(e) The prize-money will be divided *among* the members of the team.

PAGE 105

3. (a) You will find that I have *ringed* all the mistakes in red ink.

(b) No-one knew who had *rung* the fire-alarm.

(c) The curfew was *rung* at sunset.

(d) The bull had been *ringed*, and was securely chained up.

(e) The encampment was *ringed* about with cannon smoke.

4. (a) He *hung* his head in shame.

(b) "Beef, sir, is *hung*; men are *hanged*."

(c) As well be *hanged* for a sheep as a lamb.

(d) He that hath an ill name is half *hanged*.

(e) Give in? I'll be *hanged* if I will!

5. (a) Much water has *flowed* under the bridges since last we met.

(b) A stream of lava had *flowed* to within a few metres of the main gateway.

(c) The varnish has *flowed* over the surface much more readily since I warmed it.

(d) The gaoler unlocked the door of the cell, but the bird had *flown*.

(e) Then came the news that Lindbergh had *flown* solo across the Atlantic.

6. (a) We were huddled *all together* in the same tent.

(b) This is *altogether* ridiculous!

(c) My time and money have been *altogether* wasted.

(d) Keep your tools *all together* in one box.

(e) The guards were *altogether* unable to withstand the mad rush of prisoners.

7. (a) Regent Street is one of the *principal* streets of London.

(b) The *principal* of the college is Mr. Graham.

(c) That would be dishonest; as a matter of *principle* I would never do it.

(d) The *principle* of the telescope was well understood more than three hundred years ago.

(e) He has already paid fifty pounds in interest on the money he borrowed, and has not yet repaid a penny of the *principal*.

8. (a) Coal is found in seams (*i.e.*, in layers).

(b) Flat-fish (*e.g.*, plaice and sole) are caught in trawl-nets.

(c) Kerosene (*i.e.*, paraffin) is obtained from petroleum.

(d) Many towns (*e.g.*, Oxford and Bedford) sprang up at points where the river could be forded.

(e) Vegetable oils (*e.g.*, palm kernel oil) are used in the manufacture of margarine.

F. D. & C. Manual, p. 37

9. (a) The tree was struck by *lightning*.

(b) You will improve the picture by *lightening* the background slightly.

(c) *Lightening* the load on top should make the car easier to control.

(d) The *lightning* and thunder continued all night long.

(e) We could see it *lightening* in the distance, but there was no sound of thunder.

75. RATHER MORE DIFFICULT

1. (a) I have to work on *alternate* Saturdays.

(b) In case the road is flooded we had better choose an *alternative* route.

(c) *Alternate* pages of the exercise book are blank paper.

(d) We are asked to suggest an *alternative* ending to the play.

(e) I agree that my plan will not be easy to carry out, but can you suggest an *alternative* way of overcoming the difficulty?

2. (a) On one side of the square is the *council* house.

(b) If he is to help you, you must let him *counsel* you.

(c) Blessed is the man that walketh not in the *counsel* of the ungodly.

(d) *Counsel* for the prosecution then cross-examined the witness.

(e) Each month we have a meeting of the Prefects' *Council*.

PAGE 106

3. (a) What will be the *effect* of this acid?

(b) The scarcity of leather will *affect* the price of shoes.

(c) Do the new regulations *affect* you?

(d) This weed-killer will not take *effect* for about ten days.

(e) We expect the new factory to *effect* a big increase in production.

4. (a) The success of the garden party is largely *dependent* on the weather.

(b) A dictionary is a most useful book, but you should not be wholly *dependent* on it.

(c) His only *dependant* is his aged mother.

(d) If you have a *dependant* you should pay less income tax.

(e) I shall want to earn my own living, and not be *dependent* on my parents.

5. (a) The *foregoing* instructions should be made known to all employees.

(b) I am disappointed at the thought of *forgoing* my holiday.

(c) The rule for late entries remains as already stated in the *foregoing* paragraph.

(d) You will have to *forgo* smoking if you want to be a first-class athlete.

(e) With all this additional expense I shall have to *forgo* some of my pleasures.

6. (a) Men tried to fly by means of wings strapped to their arms, but they found that this was not *practicable*.

(b) Surely it is not *practicable* to send men to Saturn.

(c) The scheme that you suggest is possible but not *practical*.

(d) A lot of electricity would be saved if everyone went to bed at sunset, but is that a *practical* idea?

(e) It would be a good thing if an observatory were built at the summit; what is more, the engineers say that it is a *practicable* proposition.

7. (a) I am not *eligible* to join until I am sixteen.
   (b) Only those who have paid their membership fee are entitled to vote; others are *ineligible*.
   (c) Be sure that your examination paper is neat and *legible*.
   (d) How does he expect me to reply? His signature is quite *illegible*.
   (e) Before you submit your painting make sure that you are *eligible* to enter the competition.

8. (a) To rob a blind man is not only dishonest but *contemptible*.
   (b) He rejected my offer with a *contemptuous* wave of the hand.
   (c) It was *contemptible* of him to spoil everyone's enjoyment deliberately.
   (d) He gave a *contemptuous* laugh when he looked at my drawing.
   (e) The mob howled and raved, but the duke regarded them with *contemptuous* indifference.

9. (a) Temperatures will be well above the *seasonal* average.
   (b) An umbrella would be a more *seasonable* gift than a tennis racket during this wet spell.
   (c) Among the *seasonal* sports, skiing has become very popular.
   (d) We had snow on Midsummer Day; do you call that *seasonable* weather?
   (e) On special occasions we send our friends *seasonable* greetings.

10. (a) The fallen statue has *lain* there to this day.

(b) I *lay* down to get my breath back.
(c) I *laid* down my pen with a yawn.
(d) The ring must have *lain* in the drawer unnoticed for several years.
(e) They *laid* down their arms and surrendered.

11.(a) I have not seen her during the *past* few days.
   (b) The Levite *passed* by on the other side.
   (c) The *past* cannot be recalled.
   (d) We *passed* through Rugby at half *past* one.
   (e) The train rushed *past* us, and *passed* out of sight.

PAGE 107

76. SAME SOUND, DIFFERENT MEANING

1. (a) pause   (f) soar
   (b) stare   (g) cereal
   (c) aloud   (h) maze
   (d) draft   (i) chord
   (e) coarse   (j) berth

2. SUGGESTED ANSWERS

(1) **wholly.** Completely.
(2) **altar.** A holy table.
(3) **haul.** To pull.
(4) **hare.** A rabbit-like animal.
(5) **pail.** A bucket.
(6) **steak.** A slice of meat.
(7) **assent.** To agree.
(8) **hue.** Colour or tint.
(9) **role.** An actor's part.
(10) **muse.** To think deeply.
(11) **bored.** Wearied.
(12) **beech.** A tree.

77

(13) **wring.** To squeeze and twist.
(14) **gait.** Manner of walking.
(15) **suite.** A set.
(16) **guild.** A society.
(17) **sleigh.** A sledge.
(18) **hart.** A male deer.
(19) **manor.** A lord's lands.
(20) **teem.** To swarm; to abound.
(21) **bawl.** To shout loudly.
(22) **pique.** A spiteful feeling.
(23) **wrest.** To twist violently.
(24) **martial.** Warlike.
(25) **knead.** To work moist flour.
(26) **bier.** A stand for a coffin.
(27) **mussel.** A shell-fish.
(28) **cede.** To yield.
(29) **mite.** A tiny object.
(30) **thyme.** A fragrant herb.
(31) **mote.** A small speck.
(32) **nave.** Part of a church.
(33) **canvass.** To ask for votes.
(34) **plumb.** Upright.
(35) **bight.** A curve or loop.
(36) **ruff.** A frill.
(37) **waive.** To forgo or give up.
(38) **grater.** A scraper.
(39) **sleight.** Quickness; cunning.
(40) **sloe.** A wild plum.

⨇ LOOK THESE UP

I. (*a*) This medicine must be taken regularly.
(*b*) The lid must be replaced immediately.

2. Mr. Roy Hale thanks Miss Joyce Kay for inviting *him* to *her* birthday party, but regrets that owing to *his* recent accident *he* will not be able to attend.

3. If the phrase in parenthesis is omitted,

the sense is the reverse of what is obviously intended.

PAGE 108

77. PAST TENSE OR PAST PARTICIPLE?

(1) She *began* to cry.
(2) The money has been *stolen*.
(3) The roof was *blown* off.
(4) The doctor *came* to see me.
(5) I *saw* her yesterday.
(6) He has *given* me six pence.
(7) Were the curtains badly *torn*?
(8) Crinolines are not *worn* today.
(9) They all *went* home.
(10) French is *spoken* in Belgium.
(11) He *ran* away from me.
(12) Have you been *chosen* as vice-captain?
(13) No-one likes to be *beaten*.
(14) Who *did* this?
(15) This horse has never been *ridden*.
(16) The sun had *risen* before we woke.
(17) Have you *eaten* your cake?
(18) They *threw* confetti over us.
(19) Have you *forgotten* what I asked you to do?
(20) Several old ships are being *broken* up.
(21) Two bullocks *drew* a primitive plough.
(22) The bad apples will be *thrown* away.
(23) The generators are *driven* by steam turbines.
(24) Many pipes are being *burst* by the frost.
(25) Having *fallen* twice, he retired from the competition.
(26) They *strove* to win.
(27) Having said this he picked up his hat and *strode* to the door.

(28) These scarves are *woven* from pure silk.

(29) Until 1909 no-one had *flown* across the English Channel by aeroplane.

(30) Have I told you that I *grew* these tomatoes myself?

(31) I am sure that he *knew* he was beaten.

(32) The Egyptians were *smitten* with a plague of frogs.

F. D. & C. Manual, p. 53

78. REDUNDANCY

Words to be omitted are italicized and bracketed.

(a) St. Paul's cathedral was (*finally*) completed in 1710.

(b) When did you first (*begin to*) feel ill? OR When did you (*first*) begin to feel ill?

(c) The value of π is approximately (*about*) $3\frac{1}{7}$.
OR The value of π is (*approximately*) about $3\frac{1}{7}$.

(d) Countries of the Commonwealth are united (*together*) by their loyalty to the Crown.

(e) He is suffering from a nasal infection (*of the nose*)
OR He is suffering from an (*nasal*) infection of the nose.

(f) We revived him (*to life*) by means of artificial respiration.

(g) Betelgeuse belongs to the constellation (*of stars*) known as Orion.

(h) Draw a (*four-sided*) square (*with equal sides*).

(i) The (*very*) last pip of the time-signal occurs at (*just*) exactly six o'clock.

NOTE: There is a case here for the omission also of the word *exactly*.

(j) NOTE: There are four variants of this sentence:
Delete *A short time ago* OR *recently*.
Delete *medieval* OR *dating back to the Middle Ages*.

F. D. & C. Manual, p. 51

79. HOWLERS AND MALAPROPISMS

NOTE: Malapropisms might be regarded as howlers, but the converse does not always hold. Some howlers are faulty but ingenious deductions, whereas malapropisms are usually the result of an ignorant confusion of two words that are somewhat alike.

On this assumption, therefore, the following are malapropisms:

(a) *optimist* for *optician*

(b) *detonator* for *denominator*

(d) *meringue* for *maroon*

The remainder are howlers, with (*f*) and (*g*) showing a nice regard for etymology; (*h*) is at least in the right part of the body, and (*i*)—*doh:doh'*—is perhaps the most inspired guess of all.

F. D. & C. Manual, pp. 41 and 44

80. DOUBLE NEGATIVE

Words separated by oblique strokes are alternatives.

(a) I couldn't hear *anyone/anything/anybody*.

(b) We spoke to *no-one/nobody*.

(c) I have never used *any* of these tools.

79

(d) They didn't have *any* luck.

(e) I couldn't hear *anyone/anybody* calling.

(f) I had *no* bacon this morning.

(g) There was *none/nothing* left for me.

(h) There wasn't *any/anything* for Peter either.

(i) There was hardly *anyone/anybody* who knew me.

(j) He had written scarcely *anything* on his paper.

(k) We have not been *anywhere* near the river.

81. AMBIGUITY

(a) Whose father had been injured?
Geoffrey told Michael that Michael's (or Geoffrey's) father had been injured.

(b) Was it the fortune, or half of the fortune, that amounted to a million pounds?

EITHER *A million pounds, which was half his fortune, . . . etc.*

OR *Half of his million-pound fortune . . . etc.*

(c) The sentence obviously refers to repeated falls rather than to multiple fractures:
. . . and in several places he slipped and nearly broke his leg.

(d) *Shakespeare died on the anniversary of his birthday.*

(e) As things stand, Pierre was anti-coastguard as well as anti-smuggler; if Pierre and the coastguards were united in their opposition to the smugglers, the word *were* should be be added to the end of the sentence.

(f) The precise meaning of this sentence depends on whether the emphasis is put on *glanced*, on *Trevor's*, or on *exercise-book*.

(g) *. . . let us give it expert attention.*

(h) Jerry-building?
. . . in 1870 or thereabouts.

(i) *My friends . . .* (and leave it at that)

(j) Unless the judges were in fact singularly unobservant, the word *running* should read *in succession.*

(k) This may well be true, but the proprietors probably mean *they know that there is none better.*

(l) Unless this is one of the adventures of Superman the end of the sentence should read:
. . . when he jumped from a runaway train on which the tank was being carried.

(m) In other words:
Penalty for leaving no litter, £5.
Penalty for leaving litter elsewhere than in the basket, £5.

(n) Of the following two interpretations the second is the more probable.
It was not the rescuer himself who asked for his name to be published.
Because the rescuer had asked to remain anonymous his name was not published.

F. D. & C. Manual, p. 25

PAGE 110

82. ANTI-CLIMAX

(a) Anti-climax

(b) Climax

(c) Anti-climax

(d) Climax

(e) Anti-climax

(f) Climax, used satirically.

(g) Anti-climax, used satirically.

(h) Climax
(i) Anti-climax, used satirically.
(j) Anti-climax—to say nothing of the doggerel.

F. D. & C. Manual, pp. 26 and 30

83. ANACHRONISM

(a) Anachronism. (Pilgrim Fathers, 1620; first steamship, c. 1800.)
(b) Correct
(c) Anachronism. (Cromwell, 1599–1658; Napoleon, 1769–1821.)
(d) Anachronism. (Domesday Book, 1087; Caxton, 1422–1491.)
(e) Anachronism. (Washington, 1732–1799; American Civil War, 1861–1865.)
(f) Correct
(g) Anachronism. (Nelson, 1758–1805; introduction of anæsthetics, c. 1847.)
(h) Anachronism. (Shelley, 1792–1822; First Boer War, 1880.)
(i) Correct
(j) Anachronism. (Columbus, c. 1436–1506; formation of the U.S.A., 1776.)

F. D. & C. Manual, p. 25

PAGE 111

84. HIGH-FLOWN STYLE

SUGGESTED ANSWERS

(a) He was attacked near his home.
(b) At the end of his speech he was applauded.
(c) The bricklayers stopped work to have a drink.
(d) He was given an eight-day clock.
(e) Six persons were prosecuted for leaving litter in the streets.

(f) Many people were thrown into the icy sea.
(g) Millions of people saw the wedding by television at home.
(h) Before his death he had given generously to the poor.
(i) In winter we should feed the birds.
(j) Do not spit.

85. MISUSE OF THE WORD LITERALLY

(a) Nonsense
(b) Nonsense
(c) Sense
(d) Sense
(e) Nonsense
(f) Sense
(g) Nonsense
(h) Sense
(i) Nonsense
(j) Nonsense

F. D. & C. Manual, p. 44

PAGE 112

86. MIXED METAPHORS

SUGGESTED ANSWERS

(1) We are both in the same boat, so we had better pull together.
(2) If he pokes his nose into other people's affairs he must not be surprised if he has it put out of joint.
(3) You will never surmount this obstacle unless you face up to it (or *tackle it*) boldly.
(4) The community centre was a hive of industry, with everyone working like bees.
(5) They had an avalanche of applications that nearly overwhelmed (or *buried*) them.
(6) She is as changeable as a weathercock; whichever way the wind blows, she turns with it.

81

(7) We have had a stormy passage during the past few years, but from now onwards it will be plain sailing.

(8) The speaker lost the thread of the argument, and it was some time before he picked it up again.

(9) Once you have set your hand to the plough you should keep straight on to the end of the furrow (or *you should not look back*).

(10) If he kicks over the traces you must keep a firm rein on him.

F. D. & C. Manual, p. 45

IDIOMS AND COMMON SAYINGS

PAGE 113

87. TWO BY TWO

(a) airs and graces
(b) cut and dried
(c) tooth and nail
(d) pure and simple
(e) life and limb
(f) beck and call
(g) neck and crop
(h) neck and neck
(i) wind and limb
(j) high days and holidays
(k) root and branch
(l) all and sundry
(m) be-all and end-all
(n) pros and cons

PAGE 114

88. IN ONE WORD

SUGGESTED ANSWERS

(a) Mother was *anxious* until I rang to tell her that I had not been injured.
(b) You say that you will sell me this land; will you put that in *writing*?
(c) The sound made by the logs as they rolled off the ledge was *exactly* like heavy footsteps.

(d) I find the typewriter slow to use at the moment, but *eventually* it will save me a lot of time.
(e) She visits us only *rarely*.
(f) Mr. Banks gave me a *reprimand* in my report for not working hard enough in French.
(g) The weather was perfect; the only *drawback* was that I forgot to take my sun-glasses.
(h) Dick Turpin was hardly the kind of man to *respect*.
(i) There is only one canoe, so we shall have to use it *alternately*.
(j) Gerald wanted to be a farmer, but his father insisted on his becoming an architect. He now feels that he is a *misfit*.

89. SUCCESS OR FAILURE

(a) Kill or cure
(b) Make or break
(c) Do or die
(d) Hit or miss
(e) Now or never
(f) Sink or swim
(g) Stand or fall
(h) Neck or nothing

90. YES OR NO?

(a) No
(b) No
(c) Yes
(d) Yes
(e) No
(f) Yes

83

(g) No   (j) No
(h) No   (k) Yes
(i) Yes   (l) No

91. SAY WHICH

(a) An artist   (e) Desperate
(b) An optimist   (f) A comedian
(c) Too industrious   (g) A scamp
(d) A pauper   (h) Improvident

PAGE 115

92. TWIN SAYINGS

(a) (i) bury the hatchet
    (ii) let bygones be bygones

(b) (i) out of favour
    (ii) under a cloud

(c) (i) put his shoulder to the wheel
    (ii) kept his nose to the grindstone

(d) (i) preach to the winds
    (ii) plough the sands

(e) (i) out of his depth
    (ii) in deep water

(f) (i) take the rough with the smooth
    (ii) take the fat with the lean

(g) (i) put a spoke in his wheel
    (ii) spike his guns

(h) (i) on the horns of a dilemma
    (ii) between the devil and the deep blue sea

(i) (i) hauled (or *called*) him over the coals
    (ii) took him to task

93. CONTRASTS

(a) (i) a feather in your cap

(ii) a blot on your character (or *copybook*)

(b) (i) to strike while the iron was hot
    (ii) not to let the grass grow under his feet

(c) (i) Mrs. Wilkes barked up the wrong tree.
    (ii) Mrs. Poynton hit the nail on the head.

(d) (i) Carl takes his courage in both hands.
    (ii) Raymond has cold feet.

(e) (i) Dennis found it plain sailing.
    (ii) Martin thought it was a hard nut to crack.

(f) (i) Clive took to his heels.
    (ii) Donald stood his ground.

PAGE 116

94. TRUE OR UNTRUE?

1. (a) True   (d) Untrue
   (b) Untrue   (e) True
   (c) True   (f) Untrue

2. (a) Untrue   (d) Untrue
   (b) True   (e) Untrue
   (c) True   (f) True

3. (a) Untrue   (d) True
   (b) True   (e) Untrue
   (c) True   (f) Untrue

4. (a) True   (d) Untrue
   (b) True   (e) True
   (c) Untrue   (f) Untrue

5. (a) True   (d) True
   (b) Untrue   (e) True
   (c) Untrue   (f) Untrue

95. WORD CROSSES

```
        S                    W
        T                    I
(a)  B L I N D      (g)  M O N E Y
        L                    G
        E                    S

        S                    P
        P                    R
(b)  B U I L T      (h)  P R I Z E
        L                    D
        T                    E

        B                    A
        O                    N
(c)  C L O U D      (i)  L I G H T
        K                    E
        S                    L

        F                    R
        L                    O
(d)  P O I N T      (j)  Y O U N G
        E                    G
        S                    H

        A                    B
        L                    L
(e)  P I T C H      (k)  S H A M E
        E                    C
        R                    K

        P                    T
        E                    O
(f)  G R A S S      (l)  G L O V E
        C                    T
        E                    H
```

Other exercises of this pattern are given on page 191 of *A First English Companion*.

96. FINISH THE PHRASE

(a) Let us be quite frank about things, and put all our cards *on the table*.

(b) The news that war had been declared was a bolt *from the blue*.

(c) We are told that there are no survivors, but we are hoping against *hope* that this is not true.

(d) Most of this evidence is worthless, but some of it may be reliable; we shall have to separate the wheat *from the chaff*.

(e) You should have given us that advice earlier; it is easy to be wise *after the event*.

(f) The Chancellor has not said how he intends to raise the money, but his recent reference to income tax is a straw *in the wind*.

(g) Gambling has been his downfall. He is a brilliant man, but he has feet *of clay*.

(h) The crofters in these lonely islands are the salt *of the earth*.

(i) I shall not visit them more than once a month; I am anxious not to wear *out my welcome*.

(j) Swim the Atlantic? Have you taken leave *of your senses*?

(k) His selfish behaviour annoyed me very much, and I gave him a piece *of my mind*.

97. SPEAKING FIGURATIVELY . . .

(a) He is a pessimist, always *looking on the dark side*.

(b) Arrangements for the festival are

85

almost complete; we have only to *dot the i's and cross the t's.*

(*c*) She was willing to *go through fire and water* to save her child.

(*d*) If you are in the wrong I advise you to admit the fact *with a good grace.*

(*e*) She has been very ill indeed, but I think that she has *turned the corner.*

(*f*) The teams were evenly matched for most of the game, but the serious injury to Miller *turned the scales.*

(*g*) What he said about me is not true, and I shall make him *eat his words.*

(*h*) She *cut me dead.*

(*i*) If you invest all your money in this company you will be *putting all your eggs in one basket.*

(*j*) Cabinet ministers must expect to be *in the public eye.*

(*k*) His aunt left him a great mansion, but he soon found that it was *a white elephant.*

(*l*) You *took the words out of my mouth.*

(*m*) New motor-roads are *changing the face of* the countryside.

(*n*) If you imagine that there are no dishonest people around you, you are *seeing things through rose-coloured spectacles.*

PAGE 118

98. SPEAKING LITERALLY . . .

SUGGESTED ANSWERS

(*a*) In the middle of his lecture the speaker *forgot what should come next*, and had to search among his notes.

(*b*) Elizabeth's horse is the *thing she treasures most highly.*

(*c*) You will never get good discipline unless you *show your determination not to give way.*

(*d*) You are *blaming the wrong person* if you say that Stephen did it.

(*e*) I didn't guess; I simply *considered the facts and drew a conclusion.*

(*f*) I am anxious that you should not rush into a *job without good prospects for the future.*

(*g*) Unless we *turn our attention to the things that really matter* we shall never have this carol service ready for Christmas.

(*h*) If we are to do any good at all we shall have to *forget our disagreements, and co-operate with each other.*

(*i*) In the away match they beat us easily, but in the home match we *reversed the situation.*

(*j*) The right of way across this field has always been a *matter for dispute* between the farmer and the villagers.

99. TRUE OR UNTRUE?

1. (*a*) True   (*d*) Untrue
   (*b*) True   (*e*) Untrue
   (*c*) Untrue   (*f*) True

2. (*a*) True   (*d*) True
   (*b*) Untrue   (*e*) True
   (*c*) Untrue   (*f*) Untrue

3. (*a*) Untrue   (*d*) True
   (*b*) Untrue   (*e*) True
   (*c*) True   (*f*) Untrue

4. (*a*) Untrue   (*d*) Untrue
   (*b*) True   (*e*) True
   (*c*) Untrue   (*f*) True

5. (a) True   (d) Untrue
(b) Untrue   (e) Untrue
(c) Untrue   (f) True

6. (a) Untrue   (d) Untrue
(b) True   (e) Untrue
(c) True   (f) True

PAGE 119

100. WORD BOXES

(a)
```
M O U T H        (d)   P R O O F
A     O                I     I
R     N                T     R
C     E                C     S
H E A V Y              H E A R T
```

(b)
```
S W E E T        (e)   F L O W N
C     A                L     E
E     I                O     V
N     L                O     E
T O N G S              R I S E R
```

(c)
```
C L E A R        (f)   S W E E P
L     A                W     U
O     I                I     R
T     N                N     S
H A N D S              G O O S E
```

Other exercises of this pattern are given on page 197 of *A First English Companion*.

101. WHAT DID THEY SAY?

(a) "A cobbler should stick to his last."
(b) "You cannot have your cake and eat it."
(c) "Let bygones be bygones."
(d) "I intend to die in harness."
(e) "I have jumped out of the frying-pan into the fire."

(f) "You are flogging a dead horse."
(g) "Sour grapes!"
(h) "You are poaching on my preserves."
(i) "They are straining at a gnat and swallowing a camel."

PAGE 120

102. SAYINGS TO SUIT

I. SUGGESTED ANSWERS

(a) He is worth his salt.
(b) We always take his stories with a grain of salt.
(c) He found that he had been put below the salt.

2. (a) He draws a red herring across the trail.
(b) They were caught red-handed.
(c) She was hindered by red tape.

3. (a) She found that much water had flowed under the bridges.
(b) Advice had no more effect on him than water on a duck's back.
(c) She threw cold water on my suggestions (or said that they would not hold water).

4. (a) I prefer to pay on the nail.
(b) She hit the nail on the head.

5. (a) He hides his light under a bushel.
(b) He now sees poetry in a new (or different) light.

103. TRUE OR UNTRUE?

I. (a) True   (d) True
(b) Untrue   (e) Untrue
(c) True   (f) True

2. (a) Untrue   (d) Untrue
   (b) True   (e) Untrue
   (c) True   (f) Untrue

3. (a) True   (d) Untrue
   (b) Untrue   (e) True
   (c) Untrue   (f) True

PAGE 121

4. (a) True   (d) Untrue
   (b) Untrue   (e) True
   (c) Untrue   (f) Untrue

5. (a) True   (d) True
   (b) Untrue   (e) Untrue
   (c) True   (f) Untrue

104. DOUBLE ACROSTICS

(a)
```
C L E A N
A N G L E
T A C K S
C R E S T
H A I R S
```

(c)
```
P A I N T
U P P E R
N O B L E
C R U S E
H E E L S
```

(b)
```
C A M E L
H O R S E
A G A I N
F A T E D
F O R K S
```

(d)
```
F L I N G
A D D E R
C H I N A
T E A R S
S L E E P
```

Other exercises of this pattern are given on page 209 of *A First English Companion*.

PAGE 122

105. ...BUT THAT IS ABSURD

SUGGESTED ANSWERS

(a) A baker's dozen is thirteen.
(b) The Senior Service is the Royal Navy, not the Army.
(c) From Lapley to Dunston 'as the crow flies' is the shortest possible distance— i.e., the distance in a straight line.
(d) If Nancy took a leaf out of Mrs. Armstrong's book she followed her example, and deserved praise.
(e) The small hours are those closely following midnight.
(f) The difference between £60 and £80 is £20; splitting this difference gives an agreed price of £70.
(g) *In black and white* means *in writing*.
(h) A Parthian shot is given as one is leaving, not as an introduction.
(i) If Mr. Quayle was given *carte blanche* he was given permission to do whatever he wished.
(j) On the horns of a dilemma one has a choice of *two* evils, not three.

Other exercises of this pattern are given on page 213 of *A First English Companion*.

106. FOR INSTANCE...

(a) Shutting the stable door after the horse is gone
(b) Carrying coals to Newcastle
(c) Having too many irons in the fire
(d) Throwing a sprat to catch a mackerel
(e) Falling between two stools
(f) Killing two birds with one stone
(g) Using a steam hammer to crack a nut
(h) Killing the goose that lays the golden eggs
(i) Stopping one hole in a sieve
(j) Preaching to the converted

107. AS THE PROVERB SAYS...

(a) You can take a horse to the water, but you cannot make him drink.

(b) Don't count your chickens before they are hatched.
(c) The last straw breaks the camel's back.
(d) Everybody's business is nobody's business.
(e) Once bitten, twice shy.
(f) Familiarity breeds contempt.
(g) As you make your bed, so you must lie on it.
(h) The proof of the pudding is in the eating.
(i) It never rains but it pours.
(j) Necessity is the mother of invention.

F. D. & C. Manual, p. 97

★ REVISION

1. (a) cowardice   (d) mastery
   (b) forgiveness   (e) disgrace
   (c) boastfulness   (f) unsuitability

2. (a) selfishness   (d) reversal
   (b) resistance   (e) imitation
   (c) improvement   (f) boldness

3. (a) publicity   (d) treachery
   (b) indolence   (e) success
   (c) rebuke   (f) submission

4. (a) infrequency   (d) indecision
   (b) futility   (e) hypocrisy
   (c) pessimism   (f) inference

▥ LOOK THESE UP

1. The words available to the pupil on page 84 are as follows:

   insult, import, suspect, transport, conduct, produce, transfer, refuse, convict.

   F. D. & C. Manual, p. 23

2. *Verbs*   *Nouns*
   advise   practice
   prophesy   advice
   license

3. (a) terror   (b) ball   (c) secret
   (d) Christ   (e) cigar   (f) bronchitis

4. The letters **c** and **g** are usually hard when they come before the vowels **a, o,** and **u.**
   (a) u
   (b) e

5. The word *shady* means not only *affording protection from the sun* but also *disreputable*, or *of doubtful honesty*.
   To overlook means not only *to look down on from a height* but also *to fail to notice*.
   The fault is that of *ambiguity*.

6. (a) Euphemism   (c) Malapropism
   (b) Malapropism   (d) Euphemism

FIGURES OF SPEECH AND POETIC DEVICES

PAGE 125

108. SIMILES AND METAPHORS

1. (a) Heracles dragged a wild goat after him, for he was <u>as strong as an ox</u>.
   (b) She was leaning on a staff, the top of which was <u>like the head of an eagle.</u>
   (c) <u>Like scones on a baking-plate</u> we lay that day on the rock in the hot sun.
   (d) The plume of wood-smoke, <u>like a blue feather in a lady's hat,</u> curled from the cottage chimney.
   (e) The brightly-polished shield shone <u>as though it were the sun itself.</u>

2. (a) Surrounded by sheep, the shepherd looked <u>as though he were an idol in the midst of prostrate worshippers.</u>
   (b) A hot breeze, <u>as if breathed from the parted lips of some dragon,</u> fanned him from the south.
   (c) Silhouetted against the sunset, the bent figure of the old man <u>resembled a black wick in a candle-flame.</u>
   (d) The great aircraft rose <u>bird-like</u> into the morning sky.

(e) The earth around the gateway was trodden <u>hard and bare as a pavement</u>.

PAGE 126

3. SUGGESTED ANSWERS

   (a) I am in a groove.
   (b) We are both in the same boat.
   (c) He is rotten at the core.
   (d) We are flogging a dead horse.
   (e) He has one foot in the grave.
   (f) The sight froze my blood.
   (g) Cricket is meat and drink to him.
   (h) He is shivering on the brink.
   (i) It makes my flesh creep.
   (j) My heart was in my mouth.
   (k) You have the ball at your feet.
   (l) He swallowed the bait.

4. SUGGESTED ANSWERS

   (a) Geology is a closed book to me.
   (b) You are in a cleft stick.
   (c) He is cross-grained.
   (d) Whatever I say to him goes in at one ear and out at the other.
   (e) Her heart is made of gold.
   (f) He drew in his horns.
   (g) He has bitten off more than he can chew.
   (h) You must take the bull by the horns.

(i) You are putting the cart before the horse.
(j) He died in harness.
(k) His fingers are all thumbs.
(l) She is tied to her mother's apron-strings.

5. (a) The disappointment broke her heart.
(b) He was in a flaming temper.
(c) The robbers rained blows upon him.
(d) She was rooted to the spot with fear.
(e) He was greeted with a stony silence.

PAGE 127

6. (a) At the slightest difficulty Janet flies to her mother.
(b) The minutes crept slowly by.
(c) At last we wrung a confession from him.
(d) We must hammer out a solution to this problem.
(e) We had a flood of replies to our appeal.

7. The metaphors occurring in this exercise are as follows:
(a) His life is hanging by a thread.
(b) My geography is rusty; ....
(d) She is two-faced.
(e) The whole affair is cloaked in mystery.
(h) The problem bristles with difficulties.
(j) .... he has feet of clay.

8. (a) Simile   (d) Simile*
(b) Metaphor   (e) Metaphor
(c) Metaphor   (f) Simile
* The word *boil* is used here metaphorically.

(g) Similes   (i) Metaphor
(h) Metaphor   (j) Simile

F. D. & C. Manual, pp. 45 and 52

9. In the following sentences the similes are printed in italics and the metaphors are underlined.

(a) There were half a dozen specimens of the cactus, writhing round bits of lath, *like hairy serpents*; another specimen shooting out broad claws, *like a green lobster.*
(b) The atmosphere quivered *as if the air itself were panting*, and the purple sky was set with one great flaming jewel of fire.
(c) In this rat-infested yard was a little counting-house burrowing in the dust *as if it had fallen from the clouds and ploughed into the ground.*
(d) Through the green tree in the courtyard the sun tossed fragments of light, *like coins of silver running through a miser's fingers.*

PAGE 128

109. PERSONIFICATION

1. (a) And all I ask is a tall ship and a star to steer *her* by.
(b) Right against the eastern gate
Where the great sun begins *his* state.
(c) Slowly, silently, now the moon
Walks the night in *her* silver shoon.
(d) England mourns for *her* dead across the sea.
(e) Death lays *his* icy hand on kings.
(f) Fortune can take from us nothing but what *she* gave us.

91

(g) Poetic justice, with *her* lifted scale.

(h) Love rules *his* kingdom without a sword.

(i) Wisdom crieth without; *she* uttereth *her* voice in the streets.

(j) Accuse not Nature, *she* hath done *her* part.

2. SUGGESTED ANSWERS

(a) The bell is thought of as a gruff-voiced old man who peeps out of the bell-tower.

(b) The shop front is seen as a face, and its upper storey as a low forehead.

(c) The supporting pillars are imagined to be the failing legs of an old man.

(d) The tools are thought of as people in a crowd, jostling for position.

(e) The roses are represented as having human emotions, and as being able to speak and weep.

(f) The bridge is supposed to be a giant with great arms.

(g) In this advertisement the car engine is referred to as though it is a patient being treated by a doctor.

3.

	Inanimate	Animate
(a)	time	gipsy man
(b)	liberty	nymph
(c)	sleep	nurse
(d)	law	ass
(e)	night	bat
(f)	land	mother
(g)	life	player
(h)	virtue happiness	mother daughter
(i)	river	man

F. D. & C. Manual, p. 47

110. HYPERBOLE

(a) Hyperbole

(b) Literal statement

(c) Literal statement

(d) Hyperbole

(e) Literal statement

(f) Hyperbole

(g) Hyperbole

(h) Literal statement

(i) Hyperbole

(j) Hyperbole

(k) Hyperbole

(l) Literal statement

(m) Literal statement

(n) Hyperbole

F. D. & C. Manual, p. 41

111. EUPHEMISM

SUGGESTED ANSWERS

(a) He is a liar (*or* untruthful).

(b) She died.

(c) Mr. Borrow is short of money (*or* unable to pay his debts, *or* insolvent).

(d) My uncle was summoned for stealing.

(e) His collar is dirty.

(f) She is insane (*or* deranged, *or* mad, *or* mentally unbalanced).

(g) .... that I was sick.

(h) Mrs. Grey is ageing (*or* middle-aged, *or* elderly).

(i) Mr. Dally is lazy (*or* idle, *or* easy-going).

(j) Mr. Grabb is mean (*or* stingy, *or* miserly, *or* tight-fisted).

(k) Mr. Peacock is a braggart (*or* is boastful).

(*l*) She is incompetent (*or* unskilful, *or* unintelligent).

[NOTE: The fashion of referring to rat-catchers as *rodent operatives* and postmen as *postal distribution officers* is worthy of mention at this point.]

112. PUNS

The key words of this exercise, though all too obvious, are tabulated here for the teacher's convenience.

(*a*) Greece, grease
great, grate
colonel, kernel
adore, a door
route, root
meet, meat
(*b*) 1. feat, feet
2. *alight*, to get down; *alight*, on fire.
(*c*) pain, pane
(*d*) I'll alter him.
(*e*) *liver*—the person and the organ.
(*f*) 1. *dispense*, to deal out; *dispense with*, to do without.
2. *developing*, processing films; *developing*, expanding or growing.
(*g*) yew, ewe
(*h*) *trying*, making an effort; *trying*, hard to endure.

F. D. & C. Manual, p. 50

113. RHETORICAL QUESTIONS

SUGGESTED ANSWERS

(*a*) There is no sense in buying a car if you cannot afford to run it.

(*b*) One cannot live on two pounds a week.
(*c*) No-one wants a world without pleasure and happiness.
(*d*) A fortune is of no use to a man if he kills himself in the getting of it.
(*e*) No-one likes to have government officials prying into his private affairs.
(*f*) Money is of no value on a desert island.
(*g*) I am surely not expected to shake the rugs without making a dust.
(*h*) We must be prepared. We cannot tell when we shall be attacked.
(*i*) Our streets are much too narrow. It is no wonder that traffic is so congested.
(*j*) Children are roaming the streets until ten o'clock at night. I wonder what their parents are thinking of.

F. D. & C. Manual, p. 51

114. EPIGRAMS

1. Oral.

F. D. & C. Manual, p. 38

2. (*a*) Vulgarity is the conduct of those we do not like.
(*b*) A life of ease is a difficult pursuit.
(*c*) Duty is what one expects from others.
(*d*) A self-made man is for ever praising his creator.
(*e*) He that falls in love with himself will have no rivals.
(*f*) If a man could have half his wishes, he would double his troubles.
(*g*) The only thing experience teaches

93

us is that experience teaches us nothing.

OR We learn from history that we do not learn from history.

(*h*) Even the youngest among us is not infallible.

115. ALLITERATION

(*a*) last, lone, lamp
(*b*) stayed, stopp'd, stone
(*c*) fishes, flew, forests, figs
(*d*) way, whale's, where, wind's, whetted
(*e*) short, shrill, shriek
(*f*) pointed, pleasure
   stab, spirit
(*g*) stand, stubble, stiff
   mail, morning-prime
(*h*) sandalwood, cedarwood, sweet
   white, wine
(*i*) couched, kennel
   like, log
(*j*) Philip's, farm, flow
(*k*) know, not
   where, white
   road, runs

F. D. & C. Manual, p. 25

116. ONOMATOPŒIA

I. SUGGESTED ANSWERS

(*a*) hiss
(*b*) rustle
(*c*) rumble
(*d*) clank
(*e*) bump
(*f*) crack
(*g*) gurgle
(*h*) twang
(*i*) crunch
(*j*) crackle*
(*k*) creak
(*l*) cheep
(*m*) plop
(*n*) slap

* Also *hiss* and *spit* if the twigs are green.

2. SUGGESTED ANSWERS

(*a*) (**iv**); cracked, growled, roared, howled
(*b*) (**iii**); tinkle, time
(*c*) (**vi**); shrieking, squeaking
   Note also the effect of the f's and sibilants in the last line.
(*d*) (**ii**); lapping, crag
(*e*) (**i**); cobbles, clattered, clashed
(*f*) (**v**); broke, brittle, bright, stubble
(*g*) (**vii**); clash'd, caves, chasms, black, cliff, clang'd

PAGE 132

3. SUGGESTED ANSWERS

(*a*) (**ii**); whistled, stiff
(*b*) (**vi**); lank, clashing
(*c*) (**iii**); crackling.   Note also the effect of *question* and *arch*.
(*d*) (**v**); sound, beside, scythe, whispering
(*e*) (**iv**); enough, pant, puff.   Note also the effect of *load of links*.
(*f*) (**i**); it is the repetition of the f sound that gives the effect here.
(*g*) (**vii**); boom, beating, tin-pan gong

F. D. & C. Manual, p. 46

117. ASSONANCE

(*a*) clasps, crag, hands
(*b*) cool, soon, smooth
(*c*) so, strode, slow
(*d*) cowslip's, couch, owls
(*e*) grey, face, breaking
(*f*) light, bright, dies, dying
(*g*) we, weep, see,
   haste, away
   you, soon

(h) stream, mysterious, beneath, green, dream, deep
(i) gun, drum, trumpet, blunderbuss, thunder
(j) left, web
made, paces
through, room
saw, water
(k) we, see, ceiling
waves, pavement

F. D. & C. Manual, p. 28

118. RHYME

(a) gone
(b) lover
(c) brier
(d) veil
(e) steak
(f) stared

(g) dough
(h) flood
(i) wood
(j) plaid
(k) fume

2. love, dove
fate, weight
now, bough
done, run
height, spite
grow, though
farm, charm
wove, cove

feign, chain
blue, through
plot, yacht
form, swarm
muff, rough
flat, plait
move, prove

F. D. & C. Manual, p. 51

3. (a) **a b a b, c c d d**
(b) **a b c b, a b c b**
(c) **a a a b**

This exercise may be extended by making use of the stanzas given in Exercise 6 on page 135. The rhyme-patterns are as follows:

(a) **a b a b**
(b) **a b a b**
(c) **a b a b c c**
(d) **a a b b c c**
(e) **(aa) b (cc) b**
(f) **a b a b c c**
(g) Unrhymed
(h) **a a a b c c c b**

4. (a) daughter, water
pores, shores
(b) averr'd, bird
they, slay

F. D. & C. Manual, p. 43

119. METRE

1. reward	$\bullet$—	enjoy, contain, observe
startle	—$\bullet$	lovely, daylight, purpose
concealment	$\bullet$—$\bullet$	refusal, horizon, occasion
gratefully	—$\bullet\bullet$	marvellous, argument, plentiful
decidedly	$\bullet$—$\bullet\bullet$	community, desirable, intentional
accuracy	—$\bullet\bullet\bullet$	memorable, naturalist, delicacy

F. D. & C. Manual, p. 39

2. (a) There's the life for ever.

(b) Shallow brooks, and rivers wide.

(c) And now there came both mist and snow.

95

(d) Down to the depths of the sea.

(e) Bound and plumed with scented grasses.

(f) And green and blue his sharp eyes twinkled.

(g) How sweet the moonlight sleeps upon this bank.

(h) And there lay the rider, distorted and pale.

(i) When the trees in the orchard bend low.

(j) This is the night mail crossing the border.

3. (a) 6.6.8.6   (h) 8.8.8.8
   (b) 8.6.8.6   (i) 7.7.7.7
   (c) 8.8.8.8   (j) 7.6.7.6.7.6
   (d) 7.7.7.5   .7.6
   (e) 7.6.7.6.7.6   (k) 6.6.6.6
       .7.6   (l) 6.6.6.6.8.8
   (f) 8.7.8.7   (m) 9.8.9.8
   (g) 6.7.6.7.6.6   (n) 6.6.4.6.6.6
       .6.6   .4

IDENTICAL METRES:

Fight the good fight and
When I survey the wondrous Cross

The Church's one foundation and
Jerusalem the golden

F. D. & C. Manual, p. 52

4. 1 { As we rush, as we rush in the train
     { In a sunset of crimson and gold
   2 { Up and down the people go
     { Out upon the wharfs they came
   3 { Through the forest vast and vacant
     { Hid her face but made no answer

4 { They walked beside a hazel wood
  { I caught a little silver trout

5. (a) So in the churchyard she was laid
   (b) Sir Ralph bent over from the boat
   (c) And she may float again
       OR And float again she may
   (d) When the birds sang in the thickets
   (e) His child he did discover
       OR He did his child discover
   (f) I turned in my saddle and made its girths tight
   (g) Do ye still in slumber sit there?
       OR Do ye still sit there in slumber?
       OR Do ye sit there still in slumber?
       OR Do ye still there sit in slumber?
   (h) From the church came a murmur of folk at their prayers

PAGE 135

6. The punctuation given here is the original, but in an exercise of this kind there are of course acceptable alternatives.

   (a) By this the storm grew loud apace,
       The water-wraith was shrieking;
       And in the scowl of heaven each face
       Grew dark as they were speaking.

   (b) The wild wind rang from park and plain,
       And round the attics rumbled,
       Till all the tables danced again,
       And half the chimneys tumbled.

   (c) I love the fitful gust that shakes
       The casement all the day,
       And from the glossy elm-tree takes
       The faded leaves away,
       Twirling them by the window pane
       With thousand others down the lane.

96

(*d*) While the ploughman near at hand,
Whistles o'er the furrow'd land,
And the milkmaid singeth blithe,
And the mower whets his scythe,
And every shepherd tells his tale
Under the hawthorn in the dale.

(*e*) From my wings are shaken the
dews that waken
The sweet buds every one,
When rocked to rest on their
mother's breast
As she dances about the sun.

(*f*) There is sweet music here that
softer falls
Than petals from blown roses on
the grass,
Or night-dews on still waters between walls
Of shadowy granite, in a gleaming
pass;
Music that gentlier on the spirit
lies,
Than tired eyelids upon tired eyes.

(*g*) In his lodge beside a river,
Close beside a frozen river,
Sat an old man, sad and lonely.
And the fire was slowly dying,
As a young man, walking lightly,
At the open doorway entered.

(*h*) Gloucester, that Duke so good,
Next of the royal blood,
For famous England stood,
With his brave brother;
Clarence, in steel so bright,
Though but a maiden knight,
Yet in that famous fight,
Scarce such another.

This exercise may be used to supplement
the one on **Rhyme-patterns** (133 Ex. 3).

★ **REVISION**

1. Metaphor: (*e*) and (*h*).   Note also (*d*)
and (*j*).
Simile: (*b*) and (*i*)
Alliteration: (*c*) and (*f*)
Internal rhyme: (*d*) and (*j*)
Onomatopœia: (*a*) and (*g*)

2. Assonance: (*e*) and (*h*)
Personification: (*c*) and (*g*)
Epigram: (*f*) and (*k*)
Euphemism: (*b*) and (*j*)
Rhetorical question: (*d*) and (*l*)*
Hyperbole: (*a*) and (*i*)

* No-one can say how long the universe
will last.
The Government surely does not think that
we are all millionaires.

📖 **LOOK THESE UP**

1. (*a*) Gerald, with one of his brothers,
has gone fishing.
(*b*) Sitting at the back of the church, I
(we, they) could hardly hear the
preacher.
(*c*) She was annoyed at *my* laughing.

2. (*a*) Father said that he thought the
petrol-tank was empty.
(*b*) I asked Peter why he did not use
his own bat.

3. In the *arena* at Rome the *sand* was often
stained with the blood of the com-
batants.

IN LIGHTER VEIN

Definitions and examples of the terms used in this Section can be found alphabetically arranged in *A First English Companion*.

PAGE 137

120.

(*a*) telegraph; Anagrams
(*b*) Limerick; **a a b b a**
(*c*) A howler
(*d*) Anachronism
(*e*) Dialect
(*f*) Irish bull
F. D. & C. Manual, pp. 26, 44, 41, 25 and 43

PAGE 138

121.

(*a*) Doggerel
(*b*) Repartee
(*c*) Portmanteau words
Corbury OR Hanfield
(*d*) Pun
(*e*) Malapropism (*carnivorous* for *coniferous*)
(*f*) Parody
F. D. & C. Manual, pp. 36, 51, 49, 50 and 44

122.

(*a*) Redundancy
(*b*) A spoonerism; *a crushing blow*
(*c*) High-flown English (Journalese)
SUGGESTED ALTERNATIVE
Little Marriott, captain of the Wanders, beat the goalkeeper with a clever movement and scored.
(*d*) Mixed metaphor
(*e*) No; double negative
(*f*) Sarcasm
F. D. & C. Manual, pp. 51, 53, 44 and 45

PAGE 139

123.

(*a*) Ambiguity
(*b*) A paradox
(*c*) Anti-climax
(*d*) Hyperbole
(*e*) Irony
(*f*) A palindrome. Was it a cat I saw?
F. D. & C. Manual, pp. 25, 47, 26, 41, 43 and 46

SECTION NINE

CORRESPONDENCE

PAGE 141

124. HOW TO BEGIN AND END A LETTER

SUGGESTED ANSWERS (to which there are many alternatives):

(a) Dear Pat, (*or* My Dear Pat,)
   Yours affectionately,

(b) Sir, (*or* Dear Sir,)
   Yours faithfully,

(c) Dear Mr. Stevenson,
   Yours very sincerely,

(d) Dear Sirs,
   Yours faithfully,

(e) Dear Sir, (*or* Dear Madam,)*
   Yours faithfully, (*or* truly,)

(f) Dear Miss Fowler,
   Yours truly,

(g) Dear Uncle Paul and Aunt Susan,
   Yours affectionately,

(h) Dear Madam,
   Yours faithfully,

* or name, if the personal relationship permits.

125. SUBJECTS FOR SHORT LETTERS

Individual answers

PAGE 142

126. ADDRESSING ENVE-LOPES CORRECTLY

F. D. & C. Manual, p. 23

(a) Mr. and Mrs. N. Jackson,
   117, Foxe Road,
   BOSTON,
   Lincs.

(b) Messrs. Green and Astbury, Ltd.,
   2, Wills Street,
   BIRMINGHAM, B19 1PP.

(c) Messrs. D. R. and W. H. Fry,
   5, Stockton Road,
   DARLINGTON,
   Co. Durham.

(d) Miss Stella Edmunds,
   3, Eglantine Road,
   Wandsworth,
   LONDON, SW18 2DE.

(e) Mrs. N. J. Mills,
   The Mill House,
   MELTON,
   Glos.

(f) Misses Jill and Rosemary Wardle,
   The Grange,
   Steeple Claydon,
   BLETCHLEY,
   Bucks.

(g) The Rev. J. Ford, M.A.,
   The Manse,
      Church Street,
         READING,
            Berks. RG1 2SB

(h) Dr. C. Baker,*
   Schools Medical Officer,
   Public Health Offices,
   Rushmore Road,
      NEWBRIDGE,
         Northants.

(i) Mr. and Mrs. G. Hanson,
   284, Kingsford Smith Drive,
   Hamilton,
      BRISBANE,
         Queensland,
            Australia. 4007

* Or omit this line and begin with *The Schools Medical Officer.*

127. BRIEF MESSAGES ON POSTCARDS

Individual answers.

F. D. & C. Manual, p. 49

PAGE 143

128. TELEGRAMS

I. SUGGESTED MESSAGES

(a) LEFT SAVINGS BOOK IN SATCHEL PLEASE POST IMMEDIATELY
(b) TUESDAY CONVENIENT FOR VISIT MEETING YOU AT STATION
(c) CAN YOU KEEP GOAL TOMORROW AFTERNOON ATKINS INJURED
(d) LEFT HOUSE UNLOCKED PLEASE SECURE DOORS AND WINDOWS
(e) REGRET UNABLE TO SING TONIGHT OWING TO LARYNGITIS
(f) SAIL ORDERED RECENTLY REQUIRED FOR REGATTA ON SATURDAY

2. (a) CANNOT LEAVE MOTHER.   COMING TUESDAY.
      CANNOT LEAVE.   MOTHER COMING TUESDAY.
   (b) PLEASE RETURN KEYS.   WANTED URGENTLY.
      PLEASE RETURN.   KEYS WANTED URGENTLY.
   (c) MATCH PLAYABLE MONDAY IF WEATHER HOLDS.   WILL WIRE YOU AGAIN.
      MATCH PLAYABLE MONDAY.   IF WEATHER HOLDS WILL WIRE YOU AGAIN.

3. SUGGESTED MESSAGES

   (a) LOVE AND HEARTY CONGRATULATIONS ON THIS HAPPY ANNIVERSARY
   (b) SENDING YOUR RING ON BY REGISTERED POST
   (c) MAY I STAY FOR FEW DAYS LONGER PLEASE
   (d) GRATEFULLY ACCEPT INVITATION TO ATTEND TELEVISED CIRCUS
   (e) ROADS FLOODED ADVISE TRAVEL BY RAIL
   (f) SAFELY BILLETED FOR NIGHT OWING TO RAILWAY OBSTRUCTION
   (g) IMMEDIATE DESPATCH OF SLEEPING-BAG ORDERED RECENTLY ABSOLUTELY ESSENTIAL
   (h) FOR PREMIER TENT ORDERED YESTERDAY PLEASE SUBSTITUTE SUPER
   (i) LEFT BLUE MACKINTOSH IN MUSEUM YESTERDAY LETTER FOLLOWING
   (j) REGRET INFLUENZA PREVENTS APPEARANCE TONIGHT

F. D. & C. Manual, p. 54